Culture Wars

Other Books of Related Interest:

Opposing Viewpoints Series

Religion in America

At Issue Series

Creationism Versus Evolution

How Does Religion Influence Politics?

Is the Political Divide Harming America?

Religion and Education

"Congress shall make no law . . . abridging the freedom of speech, or of the press."

First Amendment to the U.S. Constitution

The basic foundation of our democracy is the First Amendment guarantee of freedom of expression. The Opposing Viewpoints series is dedicated to the concept of this basic freedom and the idea that it is more important to practice it than to enshrine it.

OPPOSING VIEWPOINTS® SERIES

Culture Wars

Mitchell Young, Book Editor

GREENHAVEN PRESS

An imprint of Thomson Gale, a part of The Thomson Corporation

THOMSON

GALE

Detroit • New York • San Francisco • New Haven, Conn. • Waterville, Maine • London

Christine Nasso, *Publisher*
Elizabeth Des Chenes, *Managing Editor*

© 2008 The Gale Group.

Star logo is a trademark and Gale and Greenhaven Press are registered trademarks used herein under license.

For more information, contact:
Greenhaven Press
27500 Drake Rd.
Farmington Hills, MI 48331-3535
Or you can visit our Internet site at http://www.gale.com

Cover photograph © Adrianna Williams/zefa/Corbis.

LIBRARY OF CONGRESS CATALOGING-IN-PUBLICATION DATA

Culture wars / Mitchell Young, book editor.
    p. cm. -- (Opposing viewpoints)
    Includes bibliographical references and index.
    ISBN-13: 978-0-7377-3755-4 (hardcover)
    ISBN-13: 978-0-7377-3756-1 (pbk.)
    1. United States--Social conditions--1980-. 2. Popular culture--United States. 3. Social problems--United States. 4. United States--Social life and customs. 5. United States--Politics and government--1989-. I. Young, Mitchell.
    HN59.2.C85 2008
    306.0973'09049--dc22
                                                              2007024928

ISBN-10: 0-7377-3755-7 (hardcover)
ISBN-10: 0-7377-3756-5 (pbk.)

Printed in the United States of America
10 9 8 7 6 5 4 3 2 1

Contents

Chapter 3: Is the Culture War Going Global?

Chapter 4: Is the Culture War a Matter of Economics?

Why Consider Opposing Viewpoints?

> *"The only way in which a human being can make some approach to knowing the whole of a subject is by hearing what can be said about it by persons of every variety of opinion and studying all modes in which it can be looked at by every character of mind. No wise man ever acquired his wisdom in any mode but this."*
>
> *John Stuart Mill*

In our media-intensive culture it is not difficult to find differing opinions. Thousands of newspapers and magazines and dozens of radio and television talk shows resound with differing points of view. The difficulty lies in deciding which opinion to agree with and which "experts" seem the most credible. The more inundated we become with differing opinions and claims, the more essential it is to hone critical reading and thinking skills to evaluate these ideas. Opposing Viewpoints books address this problem directly by presenting stimulating debates that can be used to enhance and teach these skills. The varied opinions contained in each book examine many different aspects of a single issue. While examining these conveniently edited opposing views, readers can develop critical thinking skills such as the ability to compare and contrast authors' credibility, facts, argumentation styles, use of persuasive techniques, and other stylistic tools. In short, the Opposing Viewpoints series is an ideal way to attain the higher-level thinking and reading skills so essential in a culture of diverse and contradictory opinions.

In addition to providing a tool for critical thinking, Opposing Viewpoints books challenge readers to question their own strongly held opinions and assumptions. Most people form their opinions on the basis of upbringing, peer pressure, and personal, cultural, or professional bias. By reading carefully balanced opposing views, readers must directly confront new ideas as well as the opinions of those with whom they disagree. This is not to simplistically argue that everyone who reads opposing views will—or should—change his or her opinion. Instead, the series enhances readers' understanding of their own views by encouraging confrontation with opposing ideas. Careful examination of others' views can lead to the readers' understanding of the logical inconsistencies in their own opinions, perspective on why they hold an opinion, and the consideration of the possibility that their opinion requires further evaluation.

Evaluating Other Opinions

To ensure that this type of examination occurs, Opposing Viewpoints books present all types of opinions. Prominent spokespeople on different sides of each issue as well as well-known professionals from many disciplines challenge the reader. An additional goal of the series is to provide a forum for other, less-known, or even unpopular viewpoints. The opinion of an ordinary person who has had to make the decision to cut off life support from a terminally ill relative, for example, may be just as valuable and provide just as much insight as a medical ethicist's professional opinion. The editors have two additional purposes in including these less-known views. One, the editors encourage readers to respect others' opinions—even when not enhanced by professional credibility. It is only by reading or listening to and objectively evaluating others' ideas that one can determine whether they are worthy of consideration. Two, the inclusion of such viewpoints encourages the important critical thinking skill of objectively evaluating an author's credentials and bias. This evaluation will illuminate an author's reasons for taking a particular stance on an issue and will aid in readers' evaluation of the author's ideas.

It is our hope that these books will give readers a deeper understanding of the issues debated and an appreciation of the complexity of even seemingly simple issues when good and honest people disagree. This awareness is particularly important in a democratic society such as ours in which people enter into public debate to determine the common good. Those with whom one disagrees should not be regarded as enemies but rather as people whose views deserve careful examination and may shed light on one's own.

Thomas Jefferson once said that "difference of opinion leads to inquiry, and inquiry to truth." Jefferson, a broadly educated man, argued that "if a nation expects to be ignorant and free . . . it expects what never was and never will be." As individuals and as a nation, it is imperative that we consider the opinions of others and examine them with skill and discernment. The Opposing Viewpoints series is intended to help readers achieve this goal.

David L. Bender and Bruno Leone,
Founders

Introduction

The Changing Nature of the Culture War

The term "culture war" was popularized in 1991 by University of Virginia sociologist James Davison Hunter, but the concept of a deep clash over values—often based on religious beliefs—goes far back in history. The term is an exact translation of the phrase *Kulturkampf*, used to describe the German government's nineteenth-century battle against the Roman Catholic church. Events in the 1920s, such as Prohibition, betrayed a religious versus secular divide in the United States. After World War II, sentiments in the United States ran against communism, which was characterized as godless. The culture war was further played out as part of the McCarthy hearings of the 1950s which sought to indict politicians, educators, and entertainers of being communist sympathizers. Hunter's *Culture Wars: The Struggle to Define America*, published in 1991, reintroduced the concept of a political struggle over values.

Traditional political analysis once focused on divisions between workers and business owners, black and white Americans, even on divisions between various religious groups. Prompted by the struggles in the late 1980s over issues such as gay rights and abortion, Hunter argues that the really important divisions in society were between "cultural conservatives" who were generally religious, and "progressives" who were more secular in outlook. Americans from all different faith traditions could be found on both sides on this cultural divide: black conservatives sided with white fundamentalist protestants against liberals of both races; Orthodox Jews made common cause with conservative Catholics on issues like abortion and education; and liberal protestants and progressive Catholics joined together in campaigns against capital punishment. Hunter's analysis was extremely influential. His book won awards and became part of the American way of talking about politics.

Hunter was not describing a new situation. American history is replete with periods of clashing cultures. The historian James McPherson has described the Civil War as a conflict of cultures, of a "Southern Civilization" defending itself against "Yankee Aggression." Political analyst Michael Barone notes that there have been various eras of cultural division in the United States, for example in the 1920s when "great political issues—immigration restriction, prohibition of liquor, women's suffrage—divided Americans according to their values." The culture war in the United States is not a novelty.

Nevertheless, the current round of the culture war does seem to be particularly long lasting. Hunter describes the new battle over moral issues such as abortion and gay rights, which heated up in the late 1980s. By the early 1990s, the war had crossed into politics. In 1992, Pat Buchanan challenged then president George H. W. Bush in the Republican primaries, largely on cultural issues. Buchanan was not able to win the nomination, but he did gain enough votes to earn a place as keynote speaker for the Republican party convention. His speech highlighted culture war themes. He accused then-Democratic presidential candidate Bill Clinton of denying the "Irish-Catholic" governor of Pennsylvania, Robert Casey "the opportunity to speak on behalf of the 25 million unborn children destroyed since *Roe v. Wade* [the Supreme Court decision legalizing abortion]." Buchanan then went on to say Clinton and his wife Hillary wanted to impose an agenda of "abortion on demand, a litmus test for the Supreme Court, homosexual rights, discrimination against religious schools" and "women in combat."

Republicans lost the White House in 1992, but they took control of Congress two years later. While perhaps not as strident as Buchanan, new Republican congressmen did use cultural issues to shore up their base in the rural Midwest, West, and South. In areas such as homosexual rights, abortion rights, and women in combat, congressional Republicans served as a sort of brake on President Clinton; throughout the late 1990s they fought to limit Clinton's social agenda. The election of George W. Bush in 2000 was seen as a complete victory for conservatives in the culture war—Bush was known to be an evangelical Christian whose religious beliefs strongly influenced his politics. When Bush and the Republicans held onto Congress and the White House in 2004, many Democrats and progressives lamented that cultural issues carried so much weight with the voters, especially those in the so-called Red States—the mainly rural, interior states that gave Bush and the congressional Republicans their victory.

The political situation seemed hopeless for the secularists and progressives who were opposed to the religious and traditional folk in the culture war, but it may have been a case of the night being darkest before dawn. The liberal author Thomas Frank wrote a book, *What's the Matter with Kansas?* (2004), decrying his rural home state's constant support for Republicans, despite the obvious damage done to small town communities by the party's *laissez-faire* economic policies. The book seems to have been a turning point; Democratic politicians began to de-emphasize their recent efforts in favor of gay rights and protecting the right to abortion. They turned instead to the economic problems being experienced by middle America. Democrats were able to turn the Republican's culture-war rhetoric against them by noting that the elites of coastal states had done well under President's Bush's program of decreased taxes and more international trade, while working people in the middle of the country were hurting. Politicians, like the newly elected Virginia senator James Webb, have attacked business leaders, noting that despite record corporate profits "the middle class of this country, our historic backbone . . . is losing its place at the table."

In the 2000s, particularly after the Republican defeat in the congressional elections of 2006, conservatives on the traditionalist right also began to question their position in the culture war. They too noted that communities were being hurt by the devotion to the free market that was characteristic of Republicans. The so-called "Crunchy Con" movement, started by Dallas-based writer Rod Dreher, is formed by conservatives who seek to live "the Good, the True, and the Beautiful," a task they find difficult in an America driven by corporate profit at all cost. They are disturbed that the "ugly suburban architecture, lousy food, chain restaurants, bad beer and scorn for the arts are defended by many rank-and-file Republicans as signs of populist authenticity." These conservatives find common cause with the people of rural America in wanting to preserve the small town way of life, even if that means going against free market, mainstream conservatives who tended to support big business in most of what it does.

Given these changes, Americans may soon see a realignment in the culture war. Crunchy cons may find common cause with fundamentalist Christians to preserve the small towns where they wish to pursue their idea of a good life. Meanwhile mainstream conservatives might find themselves allied with urban liberals as both are attacked for being part of the "coastal elite." The authors in *Opposing Viewpoints: Culture Wars* address these and other issues in chapters titled: How Does the Culture War Affect Politics in the United States? Is There a Culture War Between Believers and Humanists? Is the Culture War Going Global? Is the Culture War a Matter of Economics? What is certain is that the culture war will continue; the articles that follow may give an idea of the shape that it will take in the future.

OPPOSING
VIEWPOINTS®
SERIES

CHAPTER 1

How Does the Culture War Affect Politics in the United States?

Chapter Preface

In the early 1990s, University of Virginia sociologist John Davison Hunter noticed that traditional divisions such as religion and ethnicity were becoming less important to Americans. The true division was between those who believed in traditional values and those with more liberal or progressive beliefs. This led to Hunter's "culture war" paradigm—the lens through which the last few presidential elections have been seen. Hunter's idea led to talk of "Red State–Blue State" America, the notion of a deep division between progressive coastal states and traditional interior states.

Hunters' idea was influential, but some analysts question the usefulness of the culture war as a way of understanding United States politics. Commentators on both liberal and conservative sides still use the idea of a Red State–Blue State divide frequently, but others take a more nuanced view. In spite of seemingly polarized voting patterns, there is actually large-scale agreement on many cultural issues in the United States. Most Americans recognize the importance of family, hardwork, and general tolerance. Most take a moderate view on cultural issues. They might, for example, favor civil unions rather than marriage for homosexual couples or bans on certain types of weapons or ammunition rather than strict prohibition of guns. Americans also mix and match their positions on issues, taking the "traditionalist" position on, say, abortion but the "progressive" position on capital punishment. According to theology professor Douglas Jacobsen, "bipolar models of society surely cannot describe fairly the state of contemporary American culture and faith." Portrayals of Americans as being bitterly divided over cultural issues "are both inaccurate and harmful to the common life we share."

If the situation is mixed, why is the culture war metaphor so ingrained in the current view of politics? Part of its power is an optical illusion. In the United States's two-party, winner-take-all political system, a state that votes 51% for a conservative candidate is painted red, when it really should be seen as purple. Princeton University computer science professor Robert Vanderbei has even devised a way of mapping election data which "makes the point that most people live in rather purple counties." He notes that in his home county of Somerset, New Jersey, 52 percent voted for president Bush in 2004, and 48 percent for John Kerry, giving it a deep purple hue. The illusion of division given by maps also reflects a political reality—the American political system accentuates small differences. The two-party system typically forces voters to make a choice for a candidate that they most agree with, even if they disagree with that candidate on many issues. Political candidates tend to have a coherent position on issues, taking stances on one side of the tradiationalist versus progressive divide. A voter may agree with a candidate on a majority of the issues, or on issues they see as particularly important, and thus vote for a strict conservative (or liberal) although they themselves have a more mixed position.

All of this is not to say that real disagreements over culture do not exist. There are particularly sharp conflicts over values when public funding is involved in shaping the culture, the most prominent examples being controversies over education. The following articles address critical issues in the struggle over culture and politics; however, it is wise to keep in mind that many, if not most, Americans have mixed feelings on cultural issues. The phrase "culture war" may portray the divide in the United States too starkly.

"Why God, gays and guns? They are proxies for two distinct temperaments that divide the US like a meat axe."

American Politics Are Divided by Culture

Robert Reich

Robert Reich is a Professor of Social and Economic Policy at Brandeis University. He believes the fundamental political divisions in the United States are cultural. Conservative Americans are moral absolutists, an attitude reinforced by a feeling of powerlessness in times of great economic change. He concludes the viewpoint below by asserting that liberals and progressives can "convert" cultural conservatives by developing an economic program which leads to more equality and security for conservative, working-class Americans.

As you read, consider the following questions:

1. Which liberal ideals do the majority of the American people still support?
2. What are some differences between the way conservatives and liberals view terrorism?

3. According to Reich, why have working- and lower-middle-class Americans turned to the politics of moral absolutism? What policies does he propose to counter this trend?

This presidential election [November 2004], like all those of the past half-century, is a battle between moral absolutists and those who believe in tolerance, reason and law.

About the same portion of Americans describe themselves as being liberal (19 per cent) as believe that the world will come to an end in their lifetimes (17 per cent). Right-wingers have so effectively besmirched the term ("wishy-washy liberals", "tax-and-spend liberals", "limousine liberals"), that only a few political martyrs and masochists publicly proclaim their allegiance to the cause once championed by Franklin D Roosevelt [FDR]. The word preferred by left-of-centre types in the US is "progressive", which harkens back to the earlier Roosevelt, Teddy, a turbocharged Republican who whipped monopolists and gleefully asserted the power of the federal government.

FDR's robust liberalism focused on social justice at a time when one in four workers had lost their jobs to the Great Depression, and then on social solidarity when the US entered the Second World War. By now, much of that twin legacy has disappeared. But look beneath current political labels and you find a nation still clinging to several liberal ideals. Polls show, for example, that an overwhelming majority of Americans support social security, unemployment insurance and a minimum wage, as well as Medicare for the elderly (courtesy of Lyndon B Johnson), strong environmental protections (Richard Nixon's contribution, surprisingly enough) and a graduated income tax. Most believe that government has no business snooping into people's private lives without cause to believe that they have been involved in crime. The vast majority favour equal civil rights for blacks, women and ethnic minorities. And George W Bush's swagger notwithstanding, most

Americans oppose unilateral assertions of US power abroad. An overwhelming majority believe we should work in close concert with our long-standing allies, including France. The shrill, right-wing rantings of radio and television talk-show hosts do not reflect the views of most Americans—or the manner in which they disagree with one another.

Divisions Over Culture

The political fault-line in modern America has become cultural. It is about religion, sex and firearms (or, in the vernacular, God, gays and guns). Since 9/11 [the terrorist attacks on the US on September 11, 2001], the culture war has been extended to global terrorism. On the conservative side are Americans who attend church regularly, believe that homosexuality is morally wrong, want the government to ban abortions, take offence at out-of-wedlock births and think they have a God-given right to own any gun they wish. They also want the US to exterminate all terrorists, including anyone with terrorist leanings. Most of the people who think this way reside in rural and southern parts of the nation, towns and small cities, and outlying suburbs. They are the majority in what are now called "red states"—states that lit up bright red on the electronic TV maps late on election day 2000, when returns showed that most of their voters had cast ballots for Bush. They dine nightly on meat, potatoes and a vegetable, watch Fox News, shop at Wal-Mart, and enjoy NASCAR races and wrestling on TV. They earn between $20,000 and $60,000 a year—straddling the middle and working classes, doing jobs ranging from mechanic to clerical worker, beautician to physical therapist, and low-level managerial and technical work.

On the liberal side of the cultural divide are those whose church attendance is irregular at best, who harbour far more permissive attitudes toward sex, and think government should control gun ownership and ban handguns and assault rifles. They believe terrorism is a complex problem, requiring better

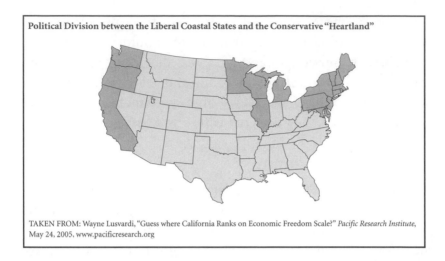

Political Division between the Liberal Coastal States and the Conservative "Heartland"

TAKEN FROM: Wayne Lusvardi, "Guess where California Ranks on Economic Freedom Scale?" *Pacific Research Institute,* May 24, 2005, www.pacificresearch.org

intelligence and more effective ways to win the hearts and minds of Muslims who now opt for suicide missions. They tend to inhabit America's sprawling metropolitan regions in the north-east and on the west coast, the larger cities and the inner suburbs. They are the majority in the "blue states" that went for Al Gore. Their tastes in food tend toward varied national and ethnic cuisines. They watch the major TV networks or public television, and play golf or baseball. They typically earn between $60,000 and $200,000 a year or they earn under $20,000. Cultural liberals tend to be both richer and poorer than cultural conservatives—moderately paid professionals such as teachers, lawyers and social workers, or else low-paid employees such as hospital orderlies, retail and restaurant workers, and hotel personnel. In other words, they are more cosmopolitan than cultural conservatives and more diverse.

Moral Absolutism Versus Tolerance

Why God, gays and guns? They are proxies for two distinct temperaments that divide the US like a meat axe. On the conservative side is a moral absolutism that views the nation's greatest challenge as holding firm to enduring values in the face of titanic economic and social changes. The common thread uniting strong religious conviction, rigid sexual norms and an insistence on owning a gun is the assertion of authority, typically by men. The task is to apply strict discipline to those who might stray from established norms, and to win what are repeatedly seen as "tests of will". Since 9/11, this has also taken the form of patriotic bravado and stubborn pugnacity. America, say cultural conservatives, must remain the strongest nation on earth. The best way to deal with terrorists is to demonstrate toughness and never waver. Better to be feared than loved; better to be consistent than appear indecisive. The tough-talking, born-again cowboy president, George W Bush, perfectly exemplifies this world-view. Bring 'em on, he says. You're with us or against us.

On the liberal (progressive) side of the cultural divide is a belief in tolerance, reason and law as central tenets of democracy. Americans who hold to this view consider all public issues to be soluble with the correct and relevant information, subjected to objective analysis and full deliberation. Religion and sex fall outside the public sphere because they are inherently private matters. A vibrant democracy must tolerate different beliefs and personal choices. Gun ownership directly affects the public sphere and, as such, is subject to regulation if there are good reasons to limit it. (As there are.) By extension, the battle against global terrorism requires that we be smart rather than merely tough. We have to get our facts straight (Saddam Hussein had no weapons of mass destruction), tell the public the truth (Iraq played no part in 9/11), apply rational analysis (our first priority must be to keep nuclear weapons out of the hands of potential terrorists) and respect international law (work through the UN and NATO, and don't torture prisoners). We also need to get at the causes of terrorism—the hate and hopelessness that fuel it. . . .

Mutual Distrust

Cultural conservatives condemn liberals as having no strict moral compass, as being "moral relativists" and "flip-floppers".

These charges predate the 2004 presidential campaign. Conservatives fear liberals will sell out because they don't know what they stand for. In fact, liberals do have strong beliefs (again: tolerance, reason, democratic debate, the rule of law), but these beliefs seem more about process than substance and do not lend themselves to 30-second soundbites. To liberals, most issues are complicated and nuanced. This attitude drives moral absolutists nuts. American liberals, for their part, worry that the right-wing conservatives are stubborn, intolerant zealots who shoot before they think. Recent history seems to bear out these fears.

Presidential elections in modern America have been about these contrasting world-views since at least 1964. Starting with Barry Goldwater's failed bid in that year and continuing through Nixon, Reagan and the two Bushes, the new right has emphasised moral absolutes and the need for authority and discipline to enforce them. By contrast, Jimmy Carter, Bill Clinton, Gore, and now [John] Kerry have focused their campaigns on tolerance, reason and democracy. Republican candidates repeatedly talk about toughness and resolve, while liberals talk about being correct and thinking problems through. On balance, toughness and resolve have proved the easier sell, especially when American voters are worried about something big.

Growing Divisions in America

What about social justice? This part of FDR's liberal legacy has been eclipsed by the culture wars. Odd, when the biggest thing voters worry about is their jobs and pay cheques, and the pay cheque (including wages and job benefits) of most Americans has been declining for two decades, adjusted for inflation. The gulf between rich and poor in America is now wider than at any time since the robber barons of the late 19th century monopolised industry and bribed the government to do nothing about it. Yet, in recent years, Democratic candidates have not dwelt on the subject. They have bought the conventional view that economic populism does not sell because most Americans still want and expect to become rich one day. That is rubbish: upward mobility has just about ground to a halt. And it's circular reasoning. Economic populism would sell if Democratic politicians explained to the public what has been happening and why. To his credit, Kerry hasn't ducked the issue. He has promised to end the Bush tax cuts for people earning more than $200,000 a year and use the proceeds to make healthcare affordable for the working class and the poor.

America is splitting into "two nations" (as John Edwards, the [2004] Democratic vice-presidential candidate, has said) because the twin forces of globalisation and technological change are rewarding the educated and well-connected, while punishing the less educated and the disconnected. What to do about this? There are solutions that do not require protectionism and neo-Luddism [opposition to technological advancement], solutions much in keeping with the liberal legacy of FDR, but too few of today's liberals have been discussing them and the American public doesn't have a clue. You hear them discussed mostly in the rarefied precincts of university towns such as Cambridge, Massachusetts, and Berkeley, California, whose inhabitants talk to one another and convince themselves that the rest of the nation must be saying the same things.

> "On election day purple independents suddenly appear red or blue. Many of them, however, are undecided until the last moment and aren't particularly happy with either choice."

Political Division Masks Cultural Agreement in the United States

Jonathan Rauch

The "culture war" hypothesis was first suggested by sociologist James Davison Hunter in 1991. Since that time the phrase has become part of American political lore; however, in the following viewpoint, columnist Jonathan Rauch investigates the scholarly literature on the supposed division between Red State and Blue State Americans. According to many scholars, Americans are more united on some issues than ever before. Jonathan Rauch is a journalist and author. His most recent book is Gay Marriage: Why It Is Good for Gays.

As you read, consider the following questions:

1. What does Rauch mean by his statement, "We do not live in a two-party universe."?

Jonathan Rauch, "Bipolar Disorder," *Atlantic*, vol. 295, no. 1, January-February 2005, pp. 102–110. Reproduced by permission.

2. Rauch asks, "Might archetypes really be stereotypes?". What docs he mean by this? How does the statement affect how we should evaluate claims of a cultural divide in the United States?

3. What are two issues on which Americans have become more united in the last twenty years? What is one issue over which they have become divided?

In 1991 James Davison Hunter, a professor of sociology and religious studies at the University of Virginia, made his mark with an influential book called *Culture Wars: The Struggle to Define America*. The notion of a country deeply and fundamentally divided over core moral and political values soon made its way into politics; in 1992 Patrick Buchanan told the Republicans at their national convention that they were fighting "a cultural war, as critical to the kind of nation we will one day be as was the Cold War itself." By 1996, in his singeing dissent in the gay-rights case *Romer v. Evans,* Supreme Court Justice Antonin Scalia could accuse the Court of "tak[ing] sides in the culture wars," and everyone knew exactly what he meant.

Red America, Blue America

In 2000 those ubiquitous election-night maps came along, with their red expanses of Bush states in the heartland and their blue blocks of Gore territory along the coasts and the Great Lakes. From then on everyone talked about red America and blue America as if they were separate countries. The 2004 post-election maps, which looked almost identical to the 2000 ones, further entrenched the conventional wisdom, to the point where most newspaper readers can recite the tropes: red America is godly, moralistic, patriotic, predominantly white, masculine, less educated, and heavily rural and suburban; blue America is secular, relativistic, internationalist, multicultural, feminine, college educated, and heavily urban and cosmopolitan. Reds vote for guns and capital punishment and war in

Iraq, blues for abortion rights and the environment. In red America, Saturday is for NASCAR and Sunday is for church. In blue America, Saturday is for the farmers' market (provided there are no actual farmers) and Sunday is for *The New York Times.*

An odd thing, however, happened to many of the scholars who set out to map this culture war: they couldn't find it. If the country is split into culturally and politically distinct camps, they ought to be fairly easy to locate. Yet scholars investigating the phenomenon have often come back empty-handed. Other scholars have tried to explain why. And so, in the fullness of time, the country has arrived at today's great divide over whether there is a great divide. . . .

Political Contests Exaggerate Differences

What, exactly, do people mean when they talk about a divided or polarized America? Often they mean simply that the country is evenly divided: split fifty-fifty, politically speaking. And so it indubitably and strikingly is. In 1979 Democratic senators, House members, governors, and state legislators commandingly outnumbered Republicans; since early in this decade the numbers have been close to equal, with Republicans slightly ahead. Opinion polls show that Republicans and Democrats are effectively tied for the public's loyalty. For the time being, America doesn't have a dominant party.

That may sound odd, given the Republicans' dominance in winner-take-all Washington. But in fact the 2004 elections confirmed that the parties are remarkably close to parity. The presidential election was tight, especially considering that an incumbent president was in the race. Republicans picked up four Senate seats, but the House of Representatives barely budged. The partisan allocation of state legislative seats (now close to parity) and of governorships (mildly favoring Republicans) also barely budged. As if to make parity official, in the main exit poll voters described themselves as Democrats and Republicans in precisely equal proportions.

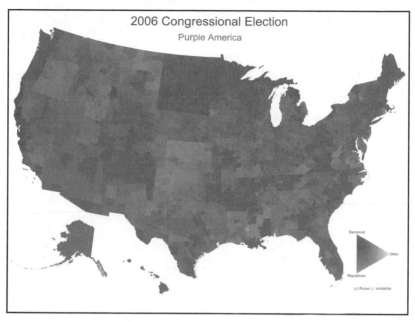

© 2006 Robert J. Vanderbei

More Independents

To political analysts, who live in a world of zero-sum contests between two political parties, it seems natural to conclude that partisan division entails cultural division. Sometimes they elide the very distinction. In his book *The Two Americas* (2004), Stanley B. Greenberg, a prominent Democratic pollster, opens with the sentence "*America is divided*" (his italics) and goes on to say, "The loyalties of American voters are now almost perfectly divided between the Democrats and Republicans, a historical political deadlock that inflames the passions of politicians and citizens alike." In a two-party universe that is indeed how things look. But we do not live in a two-party universe. The fastest-growing group in American politics is independents, many of them centrists who identify with neither party and can tip the balance in close elections. According to the Pew Research Center for the People and the Press, since the Iraq War 30 percent of Americans have identified themselves as Republicans, 31 percent as Democrats, and 39 percent as independents (or "other"). Registered voters split into even thirds.

On election day, of course, independents who want to vote almost always have to choose between a Republican and a Democrat. Like the subatomic particles that live in a state of blurred quantum indeterminacy except during those fleeting moments when they are observed, on election day purple independents suddenly appear red or blue. Many of them, however, are undecided until the last moment and aren't particularly happy with either choice. Their ambivalence disappears from the vote tallies because the very act of voting excludes the nonpartisan middle.

Internal and External Struggle Over Values

By no means, then, does partisan parity necessarily imply a deeply divided citizenry. People who talk about culture wars usually have in mind not merely a close division (fifty-fifty) but a wide or deep division—two populations with distinct and incompatible world views. It was this sort of divide that Hunter said he had found in 1991. One culture was "orthodox," the other "progressive." The disagreement transcended particular issues to encompass different conceptions of moral authority—one side anchored to tradition or the Bible, the other more relativistic. Not only does this transcendental disagreement reverberate throughout both politics and everyday life, Hunter said, but "*each side of the cultural divide can only talk past the other*" (his italics). In his book *The Values Divide* (2002) the political scientist John Kenneth White, of Catholic University, makes a similar case. "One faction emphasizes duty and morality; another stresses individual rights and self-fulfillment," he writes. The result is a "values divide"—indeed, a "chasm."

Both authors make their observations about culture and values—many of which are quite useful—by aggregating the attitudes of large populations into archetypes and characteristic world views. The question remains, however, whether actual people are either as extreme or as distinct in their views as the analysts' cultural profiles suggest. Might the archetypes really be stereotypes?

In 1998 Alan Wolfe, a sociologist at Boston College, said yes. For his book *One Nation After All*, Wolfe studied eight suburban communities. He found a battle over values, but it was fought not so much between groups as within individuals: "The two sides presumed to be fighting the culture war do not so much represent a divide between one group of Americans and another as a divide between sets of values important to everyone." Intellectuals and partisans may line up at the extremes, but ordinary people mix and match values from competing menus. Wolfe found his subjects to be "above all moderate," "reluctant to pass judgment," and "tolerant to a fault." Because opinion polls are designed to elicit and categorize disagreements, he concluded, they tend to obscure and even distort this reality.

People Are More Important than Archetypes

I recently came across an interesting example of how this can happen: In an August 2004 article Jeffrey M. Jones and Joseph Carroll, two analysts with the Gallup Organization, took note of what they called an election-year puzzle. Frequent churchgoers and men were much more likely to support George W. Bush than John Kerry. Non-churchgoers and women leaned the other way. That all jibed with the familiar archetypes of religious-male reds and secular-female blues. But here was the puzzle: "Men—particularly white men—are much less likely to attend church than are women of any race or ethnicity." How, then, could churchgoers prefer Bush if women preferred Kerry?

The answer turns out to be that most individuals don't fit the archetypes. Men who go to church every week overwhelmingly favored Bush (by almost two to one), and women who stay home on Sundays favored Kerry by a similar margin. But these two archetypal categories leave out most of the population. Women who go to church weekly, men who stay home Sundays, and people of both sexes who go to church semi-regularly are all much more closely divided. The majority of actual Americans are in this conflicted middle.

To know how polarized the country is, then, we need to know what is happening with actual people, not with cultural or demographic categories. One thing we need to know, for example, is whether more people take extreme positions, such that two randomly chosen individuals would find less common ground today than in the past. In the fifty-fifty nation does the distribution of opinion look like a football, with Americans divided but clustered around the middle? Or has it come to look like a dumbbell, with more people at the extremes and fewer in the center?

Most Americans Are in the Middle

In an impressive 1996 paper published in *The American Journal of Sociology*—"Have Americans' Social Attitudes Become More Polarized?"—the sociologists Paul DiMaggio, John Evans, and Bethany Bryson, of Princeton University, set out to answer that question using twenty years' worth of data from two periodic surveys of public opinion. They found no change in the "bimodality" of public opinion over the two decades. The football was not becoming a dumbbell.

DiMaggio and his colleagues then looked at particular issues and groups. On most issues (race and gender issues, crime and justice, attitudes toward liberals and conservatives, and sexual morality) Americans had become more united in their views, not more divided. (The exceptions were abortion and, to a lesser extent, poverty.) Perhaps more surprising, the authors found "dramatic depolarization in intergroup differences." That is, when they sorted people into groups based on age, education, sex, race, religion, and region, they found that the groups had become more likely to agree.

The authors did, however, find one group that had polarized quite dramatically: people who identified themselves as political partisans. There had been a "striking divergence of attitudes between Democrats and Republicans." In 2003 John Evans updated the study using data through 2000. He found, for the most part, no more polarization than before—except among partisans, who were more divided than ever.

> "We are indoctrinated to view people
> with the latest logo on their clothes, po-
> litically correct slogans, and phony sen-
> sitivity as virtuous people, regardless of
> their actual daily lifestyle."

Rich Elitists Seek to Impose Their Values on Traditional America

Domenick Maglio

The viewpoint that follows presents Domenick Maglio's idea of "Smuggers," a group of power-players in the media, the univer-sity, even in industry who despise ordinary Americans. These wealthy elitists, raised during the "anything goes" sixties, are de-termined to undermine the values of traditional Americans, ac-cording to Maglio. Maglio, a clinical psychologist, teacher, and a Ph.D. in human development, believes that many of the occu-pants of top positions in the United States are devoted to Marx-ism—the ideology that inspired the communist Soviet Union. In-cluded in Maglio's indictment are President and Hillary Clinton, who for the author represent the pinnacle (or abyss) of elite ha-tred for the United States.

As you read, consider the following questions:

1. Why does Maglio call the anti-traditionalist elitists "Smuggers?"

2. How did the culture war change when President Clinton took office?

3. What two controversial initiatives undertaken by President Clinton does Maglio see as evidence that he has anti-traditional values?

This cultural civil war is not a spontaneous breakdown. There has been a sophisticated strategy since the 1930s developed by a core of Marxist-humanists with the sole aim of destroying traditional countries around the world. Their plan was to wage a war from within. It wasn't until the 1990s that an overt frontal attack occurred in the United States. However, in America their progress during that time was real and subversive. The McCarthy hearings of the 1950s demonstrated the penetration of Marxist and humanist sympathizers into bureaucratic middle- and high-level government positions, higher education, entertainment, and the media.

One generation later, the anti-establishment hippies, who were to become the greatest champions of this subversive movement, set their sights on a wide range of our traditions and values. These misguided, affluent students were like children on a beach having fun digging random holes in the sand. There was no master plan. They were anointed by their frustrated professors to attack the "repressive social fabric of our society." The vision that these young radicals held was the failed utopian Marxist ideals of their all-knowing professors. The impressionable recruits were indoctrinated with these impractical notions, which had been historically shown, time after time, to be unworkable. Elitist teachers and students continue to construct these sandcastles of elaborate theories, only to see them continually washed away by the waves of time. Yet many naïve college students with little personal experience and limited knowledge of history became unknowing pawns in an ongoing cultural war. Some of these students' personal identities as adults were derived from this period of campus charade.

I will call these converts to the anti-establishment culture "Smuggers." "Smuggers" will be the term used to describe pseudo-intellectual, secular elite, Marxist-humanist oriented, antipatriotic, cultural and moral relativist, atheist hedonists who, for whatever reason, are wishing and working for the collapse of America. Smuggers are elitist know-it-alls who possess smug attitudes and are mugging us of our traditions, morals, and values.

Smuggers have been very effective in altering our perceptions and thus our values. No longer do we honor a person who has sustained doing the right thing in life—a person of good character. We have been programmed by the elite media to think of this person as self-righteous and dull. Instead, we are indoctrinated to view people with the latest logo on their clothes, politically correct slogans, and phony sensitivity as virtuous people, regardless of their actual daily lifestyle. Image is everything. Perception is reality. Smuggers have cultivated a morally shallow culture where selling one's soul for material wealth is not only acceptable, but is seen as smart. They have demeaned and continue to destroy our traditional culture. They are the enemy.

These Smuggers have used the vast power of the media, portraying men as oppressive macho brutes, mothers as dull browbeaten victims, divorce as liberating, and the youth of the era as saviors. These Smuggers, taking potshots from Hollywood pressrooms and the ivory towers of our most hallowed universities, cause damage to every institution in our nation. In one shameful generation, these me-first egotists began the process of eroding the very foundations of traditional America that had been built over hundreds of years. . . .

Americans Need to Hold Their Leaders Accountable

Our government structure set up by our founding fathers is still strong although we are not following through with our responsibility as citizens. The real issue is we are not holding ourselves and our leaders accountable to do what's right. We can no longer tolerate immoral behavior, special interest pandering and the politics of destruction. Doing the right thing for the people of America needs to be the litmus test for our leaders.

Our families, educational system, corporations, media, judicial institution, state and local government are not functioning on a high enough moral level to maintain our number one status in the world. Instead of playing the blame game we need to stand up and be heard. By each of us doing the little things necessary to straighten out this accumulated mess we can recapture our pride.

Domenick Maglio,
"End Sweeping the U.S. Problems Under the Rug,"
www.drmaglio.com.

In our contemporary age, the Culture War has morphed from defending our traditions against covert maneuvers to defending against overt full-scale battle operations. For this, we have the Clintons [Bill and Hillary, former President and First Lady] to thank, for it was not until their presidential administration that the counterculture at last felt sufficiently strong to begin imposing the ultimate phase of their strategy. Gone were the days of negotiation, of the more insidious social change resulting in the deluded Great Society of President Johnson and the ridicule phase of the 1960s. This was to be a culture based on equality, gender sameness, atheism, and cradle-to-grave entitlement coated with a veneer of hedonistic splendor. It was, in essence, new packaging for the failed Marxist concepts.

The initial Clinton administration salvo upon their election was decreed from the bully pulpit: the acceptance of gays in the military and cradle-to-grave socialized medicine. Their behavior surprised many voters, for candidate Clinton was portrayed as a centrist and moderate. The media have assisted both in advancing their positions and omitting their lies, relentlessly advancing the radical agenda set by the Clintons. Selective highlighting of daily news, focus groups, and unnamed sources are common subjective practices used by Smuggers in the media to bolster their Marxist principles. Where did all the Communist sympathizers go after the collapse of the Soviet Union? The answer is that they mutated into leftist supporters.

Confusion is a major tool in the Smuggers arsenal. Smuggers intentionally create smokescreens to hide their destructive actions. They have refined the art of pretending to honor American principles by blurring moral distinctions, distorting the truth, and outright lying, while at the same time targeting American traditions without for a moment altering their own phony smirks. Whenever their blatant biases are exposed, their reflex is to attack the opposition by accusing them of their own Smugger tactics. They are accomplished hypocrites. . . .

The anti-establishment hippies of the 1960s are presently in the halls of the Congress, the boardrooms of nonprofit and Fortune 500 companies, environmental groups, the courts, and on all levels of government, including the State Department, the Pentagon, and some even in the White House. This infiltration has escalated the frequency and intensity of the Smuggers' attacks on traditional America.

The election of G. W. Bush has frustrated the Marxists who have followed a gradual reconstruction and revisionist path to altering the American tradition. Many Smuggers have responded to the disappointment of the 2000 presidential election by reverting to spontaneous hysterical outbursts. Illegal gay marriages are sprouting one after another, there are anarchist World Trade Organization protests, and pro-Saddam's Iraq and anti-Bush rallies indicate a hatred of the possibility of a resurgence of traditional America. These actions are sporadic and do not reflect the slick, well-orchestrated policy of the Clinton years. We are at a crucial junction in the Culture War.

The Culture War is raging worldwide pitting moral traditionalism against Marxist secularism. Smuggers now believe that their victory is inevitable, an optimism that comes from the knowledge of the support they will receive from their international comrades. During the Iraqi War and the 2000 presidential elections, many U.S. elites spouted the same arguments previously pronounced by their counterparts across the ocean, the European socialists. Just as the French and German political leaders were calling us a renegade nation, these statements were translated and fed to the American public by our secular elite. In another example of international secular influence, the U.S. Supreme Court judges used international law to support the alteration of United States constitutional law—an event both unprecedented and dangerous.

Smuggers are ignorant people gleefully ripping apart their own homeland like wild animals. They believe they are geniuses who have the right to condescendingly snatch away our American principles and traditions. Our own press acts as if any pro-American foreign story would indicate a bias—even when it is relevant and true. Only anti-American information ensures their objectivity. They are as dumb as any person who burns down his own home or neighborhood to correct a perceived grievance.

Smuggers are people who believe their Marxist-derived ideals give them the right to denigrate anyone who does not believe like they do. They have exemplified the tactics of "the politics of personal destruction." The indoctrination process in schools, the media, and entertainment has anointed them superior to anyone who is morally upright, hardworking, and patriotic. Whenever a patriot expresses traditional viewpoints in a room with two or more Smuggers, the Smuggers will raise their eyebrows to communicate disdain to each other that they are in the company of an inferior thinking person. The power they possess does not come from numbers or ideas; it comes from their sniper tactics.

These Smuggers are slick guerrilla goons who exploit their positions to cleverly undermine our traditions and incessantly spread their propaganda. These subversive tactics can only be repelled by recognizing the phony smiles and condescending attitudes. These warning signs should alert us to the coming attack on our values. Only through greater awareness will we be able to ward off these misguided, ignorant pawns of anti-Americanism. Smuggers must be identified and neutralized to preserve our nation.

| "The emotional resonance of Reagan's; persona rested on a profound rejection of the moral claims of the interventionist political class, whom the president equated with the cosmopolitan intelligentsia."

Conservative Politicians Encourage Resentment Against Liberal Policy Makers

David A. Horowitz

In this viewpoint, history professor David A. Horowitz outlines how Presidents Reagan and George H. W. Bush used the public's mistrust of government to win elections. These politicians capitalized on fears of "social engineering" and moral permissiveness highlighted by leaders of the Religious Right. By expressing a strong belief in individual responsibility, as well as skepticism that government bureaucrats could solve the nation's problems, both Reagan and his former vice-president managed to win the majority of voters.

David A. Horowitz, from *America's Political Class under Fire: The Twentieth Century's Great Culture War*, New York: Routledge, 2003, pp. 204–207. Copyright © 2003 by David A. Horowitz. All rights reserved. Reproduced by permission of Routledge/Taylor & Francis Books, Inc., and the author.

As you read, consider the following questions:

1. When did evangelical ministers start to gain political influence? What politician was one of the first beneficiaries of fundamentalist Christian support?

2. Did Reagan's actions as governor of California match the beliefs he declared in his speeches? Why might there be a difference between his actions and his rhetoric?

3. What famous case allowed George H. W. Bush (as a presidential candidate) to play on fear of crime?

Secularism, hedonism, and permissiveness were the main targets of the social crusade inaugurated in the late-1970s by evangelical and fundamentalist Protestant ministers Jerry Falwell and Pat Robertson. The main beneficiary of Christian Right political involvement was former California governor, Ronald Reagan. As unemployment rose to 7 percent, inflation ballooned to 13.5 percent, and interest rates soared above 20 percent in 1980, Reagan leaped onto the post-Watergate political stage. Long known for his anticommunist views, the affable Californian had built a public persona on opposition to government bureaucrats and planners. During his televised endorsement of Barry Goldwater in 1964, Reagan had warned that "government can't control the economy without controlling the people." The governor continued to oppose Great Society social spending. "It should be obvious by now," he told Republicans across the race-conscious South in 1967, "that a self-appointed group of experts operating out of either Washington or Sacramento cannot have all the answers to the problems that beset us."

Ronald Reagan Attacks the Liberal Elite

Speaking before the largest political fundraising gathering in South Carolina history in 1967, Reagan accused the Democratic Party of betraying its supporters by deciding "that a few men in Washington knew better than we do what is good for us and know better than we do how to spend all our money." Voters would have to remove "the little intellectual elite" leading the country, the governor told a Republican fundraising rally in Louisville, in order to honor the "forgotten men and women who work and support the communities and pay for all the social experimenting." Addressing 1,200 guests of the Economic Club of New York early in 1968, Reagan lamented that Americans were experiencing "a feeling of helplessness, a feeling that government is now a separate force beyond the people's control."

In eight years as California governor, Reagan more than doubled the state budget deficit, tightened environmental regulations, and generously increased public education spending. Yet in 1980 the Republican presidential candidate campaigned as an outsider representing ordinary people in the fight against "special interests" and untrustworthy cultural elites. Reagan claimed that a career of film acting had taught him to be in touch with audiences so that his speeches rang with "certain basic truths" recognized by average citizens. He rejected the moral relativism of academics who saw "just shades of gray in a world where discipline of any kind is an intolerable interference with the right of the individual." It was foolish to deny there were any absolutes, a "black and white of right and wrong," the governor informed the California Federation of Republican Women in 1970. Ten years later, Reagan sought to lead Americans into "an era of national renewal" to "revitalize the values of family, work, and neighborhood" and free citizens from government bureaucracy.

As historian Christopher Lasch suggested, the Republican candidate never acknowledged how consumer capitalism eroded the traditional values he invoked. Nor did Reagan reveal the extent to which his conservative views resonated with the free market ideology of the corporate-financed think tanks and foundations calling for less government in the 1970s. Nevertheless, by equating liberal programs with inegalitarian

Ronald Reagan Expresses Wariness of Government "Do-Gooders"

[P]ublic servants say, always with the best of intentions, "What greater service we could render if only we had a little more money and a little more power." But the truth is that outside of its legitimate function, government does nothing as well or as economically as the private sector of the economy. What better example do we have of this than government's involvement in the farm economy over the last thirty years. One-fourth of farming has seen a steady decline in the per capita consumption of everything it produces. That one-fourth is regulated and subsidized by government.

Ronald Reagan, "A Time for Choosing,"
speech at Republican Party Convention, October 27, 1964.
www.reagan.utexas.edu.

attempts to impose racial preferences and "reverse discrimination," the former governor succeeded in attacking rule by interventionist political intellectuals and knowledge professionals while avoiding the nasty connotations of race-baiting. The cheerful and optimistic Californian built a powerful electoral coalition by promising to protect both working-class voters and corporate interests from excessive government regulation, wasteful welfare spending, and burdensome taxation. As Reagan rode to easy victory in 1980 against the hapless Jimmy Carter, exit polling showed that one-fourth of Democrats and 41 percent of union households voted Republican. The new president's inaugural address sustained the populist distinction between ordinary people and "government by an elite group." Promising to curb the size and influence of the "federal establishment," Reagan insisted that working people were "a special interest group" that had been "too long neglected." Government itself had become the problem.

Confidence in Ordinary People

Reagan bonded with supporters by attributing common sense to ordinary people in contrast to the impractical ideologies he assigned to political intellectuals and cultural guardians. "This administration is motivated by a political philosophy that sees the greatness of America in you, her people, and in your families, churches, neighborhoods, communities," he told a 1983 meeting of the National Association of Evangelicals in Orlando, Florida. The president portrayed liberal policy planners and social interventionists as creatures of a spiritually empty and materialist Marxist vision. The national renaissance would not be achieved "by those who set people against people, class against class, or institution against institution," he assured the Conservative Political Action Conference in 1981. Reagan teased the financial technicians of the International Monetary Conference by suggesting that an economist was "the only professional who sees something working in practice and then seriously wonders if it works in theory." But the president was serious in 1985 when he introduced a simplified federal tax structure (lowering rates on the affluent but eliminating many deductions) and attacked "Washington sophisticates" and "special interest lobbyists" for opposing the plan supposedly backed by ordinary citizens.

The emotional resonance of Reagan's persona rested on a profound rejection of the moral claims of the interventionist political class, whom the president equated with the cosmopolitan intelligentsia. Average Americans "held true to certain beliefs and principles" dismissed by intellectuals as "hopelessly out of date, utterly trite, and reactionary," he told the Conservative Political Action Conference in 1985. Reagan asserted that cultural experimenters believed that "only the abnormal was worthy of emulation," while they viewed religious devotion and adherence to traditional verities as "primitive" and "antimodern." Such thinkers saw people "only as members of groups," not as individuals. The president insisted that Americans either must side with "pipe dreamers and margin scribblers" or place their faith "in the common sense of the people." Taking aim at social welfare and civil rights policies most strongly identified with Great Society political intellectuals, Reagan followed through on his commitment to lower taxes, initiated major cuts in social services, restrained the regulatory agencies, opposed busing and mandated efforts at school desegregation, reduced budgets for legal services to the poor, substantially curtailed the implementation of affirmative action, and stacked the U.S. Commission on Civil Rights and Equal Employment Opportunity Commission with conservative appointees.

A Winning Strategy

Republican presidents of the 1980s skillfully exploited hostility to the interventionist political intelligentsia. When Reagan sought a second term in 1984, he faced a strong contender in former senator and Carter vice-president Walter F. Mondale, a career liberal with strong ties to organized labor, the civil rights movement, and feminist groups. Yet Mondale appeared overly beholden to women's rights lobbies when he named Geraldine A. Ferraro, a relatively inexperienced member of the House, as his vice-presidential running mate. The Minnesotan suffered an additional blow when he indicated that he might approve tax increases to reduce spiraling budget deficits, a gesture that backfired because it appeared to question the nation's ability to generate strong economic growth without inflation or the intrusion of technocrats. Mondale also failed to assure working-class voters that they would not shoulder added revenue burdens in a tax system that favored both the rich and special interest groups. Amid increased prosperity and national optimism, Reagan and Vice President George H. W. Bush eased to victory with 59 percent of the popular vote.

When Bush ran for president on his own account in 1988, he guaranteed voters that he would adhere to Reaganomics and supply-side financing by opposing any tax increases or unnecessary growth in the public sector. Once again, the Republicans were challenged by an impressive rival in Massachusetts governor Michael S. Dukakis. A Greek American who taught university seminars on public administration and the efficient use of government, Dukakis claimed to have restored his state economy through astute fiscal management and recruitment of new businesses. Facing a deficit hawk who also talked about the need to create economic opportunity for working people, the Bush camp shifted the debate away from bread-and-butter issues and tax-and-spend liberals. Instead, White House strategists mounted a brilliantly conceived attack on the cultural mores and reformist tendencies of New Class professionals and liberal political insiders.

Playing upon a tangled set of sentiments concerning crime, race, patriotism, and cultural permissiveness, Bush focused on Dukakis's opposition to the death penalty, his veto of a state bill to require public school teachers to lead students in the Pledge of Allegiance, his administration of a convict furlough program, and his membership in the rights-oriented American Civil Liberties Union. The governor's positions on capital punishment and compulsory flag saluting reflected a profound reverence for constitutional protections and procedures. Yet many Americans wondered if affluent liberals and technocrats excessively fixated on process and individual rights and ignored the need to enforce widely shared moral commitments. Social conservatives believed that patriotism was a traditional obligation that should be taught in the schools if the excesses of fashionable self-indulgence were to be avoided. Support of the death penalty, in turn, reflected widespread frustration with the perceived failures of the criminal justice system and anxiety over lawlessness as a symptom of social disorder.

Playing on Fear of Crime

The Bush campaign climaxed when a Republican political action committee aired a television commercial dramatizing the case of Willie Horton, an African American convict serving a murder sentence in Dukakis's Massachusetts. Released on a weekend furlough permissable under state law, Horton had raped a white woman in Maryland and brutally beaten her fiancé. The widely distributed video implied that rights-oriented liberals lacked common sense as well as reverence for traditional values. It underscored the suspicion that interventionist political intellectuals and government planners were more concerned with social experiment and the perogatives of criminals than with protecting the safety, interests, and values of ordinary citizens. "I don't understand the type of thinking," Bush told a North Carolina rally, "that lets first-degree murderers who haven't even served enough time to be eligible for parole out on parole so they can rape and plunder again, and then isn't willing to let the teachers lead the kids in the Pledge of Allegiance." The vice-president described Dukakis as a "know nothing, believe nothing, feel nothing candidate," an "ice man."

Exploitation of these powerful social issues enabled George H. W. Bush to rebound from a seventeen-point polling deficit in 1988 to an easy Election Day victory over the pragmatic but cerebral Dukakis. The new administration soon clarified its distance from the social interventionists and planning professionals of the Democratic Party. "The New Paradigm," an address delivered in 1990 by Bush policy planning assistant James Pinkerton, laid to rest the reformist aura of the Lyndon Johnson years. The Great Society was "a continuing, if well-intentional failure," stated Pinkerton, because it falsely assumed "that experts, wise bureaucrats in league with university professors and politicians," could "administer supply and demand, prosperity and equality, from an office building far away."

Periodical Bibliography

The following articles have been selected to supplement the diverse views presented in this chapter.

Michael Barone — "A History of Culture Wars," *U.S. News & World Report*, August 1, 1994.

Patrick J. Buchanan — "Keynote Speech—Republican National Convention," *Patrick J. Buchanan*, August 17, 1992. www.buchanan.org.

Connection: New England's Journal of Higher Education & Economic Development — "Culture War?" Summer 1997.

E. J. Dionne, Jr. — "Why the Culture War Is the Wrong War," *Atlantic Monthly*, January/February 2006.

Jay Greene and Mike France with David Kiley — "Culture Wars Hit Corporate America," *Business Week*, May 23, 2005.

George Hodak — "Judges in the Culture Wars Crossfire," *ABA Journal*, October 2005.

Jonathan B. Imber — "Doubting Culture Wars," *Society*, September/October 2001.

Randy Lee — "Recognizing Friends Amidst the Rubble: Seeking Truth Outside the Culture Wars," *Widener Law Journal*, 2004.

Rick Perlstein — "He Discovered the Culture Wars, Then Reported Behind the Lines," *Columbia Journalism Review*, November/December 2004.

Steven Schultz — "Mathematical View Sees Beyond Conventional Election Coverage," *Princeton Weekly Bulletin*, November 22, 2004.

Steven Selden — "Who's Paying for the Culture Wars?" *Academe*, September/October 2005.

CHAPTER 2

Is There a Culture War Between Believers and Humanists?

Chapter Preface

The culture war has always been associated with religion. The vast majority of Americans who side with "traditional values" are religious. Moreover, those on the conservative side of the culture war tend to belong to more fundamentalist branches of their faith, whether they are Evangelical Protestants, traditionalist Catholics, or Orthodox Jews. Many liberal and progressive Americans also have a strong religious faith, but their ideas of religion tend to be more open-ended; they do not typically believe in strict doctrines or rigid religious practices. While liberals and conservatives certainly clash within their various churches, the real culture clash occurs when religion enters the public sphere. Arguments over such issues as prayer in public schools, the teaching of evolution, and displays of religious symbols in public places have been repeated again and again, with no permanent resolution in sight.

Conservative Christians (often called the Religious Right) see themselves as on the defensive in the war over religion in public. Beginning as long ago as the 1920s, fundamentalists have seen such public policies as the teaching of Charles Darwin's theory of the evolution of species (including humans) as a threat to their religious beliefs. Conservative Protestants experienced public humiliation over this issue at the famous "Scopes Monkey Trial" of 1925, after which they "withdrew from the public spotlight to build their own separate institutions," according to sociologists Robert Woodberry and Christian Smith. The 1963 Supreme Court decision to ban collective prayer in public schools added to traditional Christians' feeling they were being attacked. Today, claim some Christians, the bias against the religion of the majority of Americans is so great that all sorts of beliefs—from Islam to Native American religions—can be discussed in public schools while the pivotal role of Christianity in American history is ignored. The struggle extends beyond the schools; the year-end holidays bring complaints of a "War on Christmas" because major private corporations and government agencies are eliminating all mention of specific holidays.

To counter these developments, Christian fundamentalists have emerged from their self-exile from politics and joined with conservative Catholics to form organizations which promote religion in the public sphere. They have also helped candidates with fundamentalist views gain offices on local and state school boards. Such groups have had some success in seeing their policies implemented. Conservative members of the Kansas State School Board have promoted the teaching of "creation science," which detractors say is nothing but a cover for non-scientific, anti-evolution dogma. Also, politicians are sensitive to the use of public money to fund arts and humanities programs which are considered religiously offensive.

These developments worry secularists—people who believe religion should be a private matter. They see the strict separation of church and state as being eroded by the political activity of religious fundamentalists. They have formed organizations, such as People for the American Way, to counter the perceived threat from religious conservatives. The record of these new battles between secularists and the Religious Right is mixed; while there have been few results in the courts which allow an increased role for religion, public elected officials are under pressure to make public education and other areas of government action acceptable to the traditionally religious. As social commentator Gertrude Himmelfarb points out, conservative Christian believers are a "dissident, minority culture that can be disproportionately influential."

Conservatives and secularists will continue the struggle into the foreseeable future. The Supreme Court now has four conservative Roman Catholic justices (Clarence Thomas, Antonin Scalia, Samuel Alito, and Chief Justice John Roberts) which might provide an opportunity for traditionalists to "roll back" what they see as anti-religious, anti-Christian rulings. In the culture war, the battle between secularist progressives and religious traditionalists will be a long one. The following articles present some areas of possible conflict.

> "Through the years the humanists succeeded in a big way. They have made significant inroads into many of our cultural institutions, not least the education system."

Humanists Have Expelled Christianity from the Classroom

David Limbaugh

In this viewpoint, David Limbaugh, a conservative columnist and attorney, describes how humanism has come to be taught in America's schoolrooms. Humanism is a philosophy that is skeptical of the existence of God and concentrates on human conditions in the here and now. Far from being a neutral worldview, according to Limbaugh, it is hostile to traditional religion, especially Christianity. Because of the dominance of humanism in the schools, students are being taught a false view of American history and society. Moreover, because our political institutions are based on Christian thought, according to Limbaugh the bias against Christianity endangers Americans' liberties.

David Limbaugh, from *Persecution: How Liberals Are Waging War Against Christianity*, Washington, DC: Regnery, 2003, pp. 65–70. Copyright © 2003 Henry Regnery Company. All rights reserved. Reproduced by special permission of Regnery Publishing Inc., Washington, DC.

As you read, consider the following questions:

1. When did humanism start to make inroads in American education?

2. Why does Limbaugh claim that humanism is a religious worldview?

3. How does the Thanksgiving celebrated by the Pilgrims differ (according to Limbaugh) from the version now taught in America's public schools?

To understand the secular values the education establishment is actively promoting in our public schools, we need to review the humanistic movement in America that began in the nineteenth century. In 1876, former rabbi Dr. Felix Adler helped to establish the Society for Ethical Culture in New York City. This led to many other such societies that were later unified in the American Ethical Union, also founded by Adler, in 1889. The American Ethical Union was a seedbed for what would become "secular humanism," a philosophy that teaches that God does not exist, and that man is perfectible, self-sufficient and the measure of all things. By the early twentieth century, humanism had already begun to manifest itself in America's cultural institutions and public schools. In 1929, a former Baptist, then Unitarian preacher, Charles F. Potter, founded the First Humanist Society of New York. The next year, he wrote *Humanism: A New Religion*, which stated flatly, "Education is thus a most powerful ally of Humanism, and every American public school is a school of Humanism. What can the theistic Sunday-schools, meeting for an hour once a week, and teaching only a fraction of the children, do to stem the tide of a five-day program of humanistic teaching?"

If humanism crept in as a natural byproduct of the secularism successfully promoted by Horace Mann in the public schools in the late nineteenth century, by the time America was in the Great Depression, it had achieved a level of mainstream acceptance in American culture. In 1933 the *Humanist*

Manifesto was published and signed by thirty-four national figures, bringing humanism to a level of prominence in American culture. Educator John Dewey was among the signatories of this document that rejected traditional Christian beliefs and endorsed, as an alternative, those of naturalism, materialism, rationalism, and socialism. The *Humanist Manifesto* expressed the humanists' goal: "to evaluate, transform, control, and direct all institutions and organizations by its own value system." As one writer has noted, the humanists' stated purpose was to effect a cultural revolution by substituting humanism for Christianity as the cultural foundation of America.

Through the years the humanists succeeded in a big way. They have made significant inroads into many of our cultural institutions, not least the education system. In education, humanism became a great motivator, the great cause to which educators could devote their lives by influencing students, and also provided a coherent organizing principle, giving education a larger purpose. John Dewey's books were practically mandatory reading in teacher training colleges, making humanism the mainstream philosophy of public education. Humanism, not posing as a traditional religion, could enforce its own values under the guise of neutrality and without much scrutiny. Its precepts have come to inform the entire public school curriculum, as meticulously documented by Samuel L. Blumenfeld's *NEA: Trojan Horse in American Education*. Yet, the strict separationists don't call education's endorsement of this values-driven worldview an encroachment on the Establishment Clause. That they don't reveals that their true interest lies in promoting secular values, rather than enforcing a strict separation of church and state.

Indeed, secular humanism is values-based. John Dewey described it as our "common faith." Canada's Christian Heritage Party leader Ron Gray observed, "We must not make the mistake of thinking that 'secular' means 'neutral.' Secularism is a religious worldview, the most bigoted faith on earth: its goal is to extirpate every other faith." The first *Humanist Manifesto* referred to humanism as a religion. Even the United States Supreme Court, in *Torcaso v. Watkins* (1961), recognized secular humanism as a religion: "Among religions in this country which do not teach what would generally be considered a belief in the existence of God, are Buddhism, Taoism, Ethical Culture, Secular Humanism and others."

Humanist principles cannot fairly be reconciled with Christian ones—they are "radically at war with biblical religion." [According to author Robert L. Waggoner,] [h]umanists themselves make this quite clear. In *Humanist Manifesto III*, released in 2003, they affirm their beliefs in the self-existence of nature, a denial of the supernatural, and the "finality of death." In fact, humanism subscribes to the notion that man's idea of religion itself was sparked by his interaction with the natural environment, as opposed to the distinctly Judeo-Christian view that God revealed Himself to man. Biologist and humanist Julian Huxley called it "Religion without Revelation." Moreover, humanism "affirm[s] that moral values derive their source from human experience" and [not from God].

History Revisionism: Excising Christianity

It's one thing to prohibit public schools from endorsing a particular religion, but does that mean that all references to Christian influences in our history should be expunged from our textbooks? Federal law is clear that schools may teach *about* religion, and schools are certainly not required to falsify history and delete Christianity from our heritage. Nevertheless, there has been a conscious decision to sanitize our history textbooks of information concerning the dominant presence of Christianity in colonial culture.

When Noah Webster wrote his *History of the United States*, published in 1832, he could state, "Almost all the civil liberty now enjoyed in the world owes its origin to the principles of the Christian religion. . . . The religion which has introduced

Humanism's View of Religion

For evolutionary humanism, gods are creations of man, not vice versa. Gods begin as hypotheses serving to account for certain phenomena of outer nature and and inner experience: they develop into more unified theories, which purport to explain the phenomena and make them comprehensible; and they end up being hypostatized as supernatural personal beings capable of influencing the phenomena. As theology develops, the range of phenomena accounted for by the god-hypothesis is extended to cover the entire universe, and the gods become merged in God.

Julian Huxley, "The Coming of the New Religion of Humanism,"
The Humanist, *January-February 1962.*

civil liberty is the religion of Christ and His Apostles, which enjoins humility, piety, and benevolence; which acknowledges in every person a brother or sister and a citizen with equal rights. This is genuine Christianity, and to this we owe our free constitutions of government." As a leading American educator of his time, he could rest assured that this view was also routinely taught in the schools. It is not taught today.

The New Jersey Department of Education removed references to the Pilgrims and the *Mayflower* from its history standards for school textbooks. The problem is that "Pilgrim" suggests religion, according to Brian Jones, vice president for Communications and Policy at the Education Leaders Council in Washington. Other historical events involving Christian worship or expression are also often taboo. "It's getting more difficult," said Jones, "to talk about the Bible and the Puritans"—or at least to talk about them accurately.

A study by New York University psychology professor Paul Vitz documented the purging of religion from public school textbooks. In examining sixty widely used social studies textbooks (used by eighty-seven percent of public school students), Vitz didn't find one that imparted the spirituality of the Pilgrims. Vitz wrote, "Are public school textbooks biased? Are they censored? The answer to both is yes, and the nature of the bias is clear: Religion, traditional family values and many conservative positions have been reliably excluded from children's textbooks. . . . There is not one story or article in all these books in which the central motivation or major content is connected to Judeo-Christian religion. . . . In grades one through four these books introduce the child to U.S. society—to family life, community activities, ordinary economic transactions, and some history. None of the books covering grades one through four contains one word referring to any religious activity in contemporary American life." Vitz concluded, "Religion, especially Christianity, has played and continues to play a central role in our culture and history. To neglect to report this is simply to fail to carry out the major duty of any textbook writer to tell the truth."

One book had thirty pages on the Pilgrims, including the first Thanksgiving. But there was not a single reference to religion, even as part of the Pilgrims' lives. Another textbook described the Pilgrims simply as "people who make long trips." Another said that after their first year, the pilgrims "wanted to give thanks for all they had," omitting that they were thanking God. Dr. Vitz said, "It is common in these books to treat Thanksgiving without explaining to whom the Pilgrims gave thanks. . . . The Pueblo [Indians] can pray to Mother Earth, but Pilgrims can't be described as praying to God—and never are Christians described as praying to Jesus. . . ."

Indeed, many public schools now portray Thanksgiving as a multicultural harvest feast in which American colonists gave thanks to Indians. But this is "feel-good" myth. In fact, the Pilgrims' earliest thanksgiving celebrations, beginning in 1621, were expressing gratitude to the God of the Bible. When they landed at Plymouth in December 1620, the severity of the winter killed almost half of their people. But the next autumn's harvest was plentiful and in gratitude they held a three-day celebratory feast of thanksgiving to God. In 1623, Massachusetts Governor William Bradford set apart a day for prayer and fasting to praise God for the rain that had saved the colony's crops from a threatening drought.

President George Washington's first proclamation was the declaration of a national Thanksgiving Day, explicitly devoted to giving thanks to God. But Thanksgiving wasn't celebrated as an annual holiday until President Lincoln established it as such. In his Thanksgiving Proclamation setting aside the last Thursday of November as a national holiday he wrote, "I do therefore invite my fellow citizens in every part of the United States, and also those who are at sea and those who are sojourning in foreign lands, to set apart and observe the last Thursday of November next, as a day of Thanksgiving and Praise to our beneficent Father who dwelleth in the Heavens."

Despite the undeniable Christian origins and purpose of Thanksgiving Day, in 1995 the National Education Association passed a resolution affirming its belief "that Thanksgiving is the recognition of unity and the rich American diversity that was embodied in the settlement of America. This Association further believes that this national holiday must celebrate the coming together of peoples and the inclusion of all immigrants as a part of this great diverse country." Whatever the merits of celebrating "diversity," as the education establishment uses that term, there is no excuse for misleading students about the stated historical purpose of the Thanksgiving holiday. And such rewriting of history is dangerous. If Noah Webster is right that the source of our freedom is the Christianity that shaped colonial America, then to deny students that perspective is to make students less well prepared to defend our liberty, or even recognize when it is being infringed.

> "[A] New Yorker worried that schools were actually evolving 'a strange new hybrid religion,' as distasteful to Jews as it was to other faiths."

Conflicts Over Prayer in Schools Are Deeply Rooted in American History

Jonathan Zimmerman

The clash over religion in public schools is emblematic of the culture wars. In this viewpoint, historian Jonathan Zimmerman describes the battle over the Supreme Court decision in McCollum v. Board of Education (1948). The decision outlawed so-called "released-time" religious education in which pupils were allowed to attend religious instruction in the school building during school hours. Some school districts refused to follow the decision. Civic groups tried to avoid the issue by devising a "common core" religious curriculum that could be taught in the public schools, leading to disputes between various religious groups. These battles continued over the middle decades of the twentieth century.

As you read, consider the following questions:

1. What were some responses by school districts to the Supreme Court's banning of "released-time" religious education in *McCollum v. Board of Education*?

2. How did international political conditions affect the battle over religious education in American schools?

3. Why did Jews and Fundamentalists object to the "common-core" idea of religious education?

"It is safe to say that no decision by the highest court in the land has ever caused greater consternation than this one," pronounced the Rev. W. T. Smith, of Peoria, Illinois, in March 1948. "It is equally safe to say that the issue is not closed." Here Smith joined the rising chorus of American outrage at the Supreme Court's decision in *McCollum v. Board of Education*. Hundreds of churches and school districts had quickly announced that they would continue their released-time operations no matter what the Court said. In other schools the decision rejuvenated efforts to infuse the regular curriculum with religious instruction. Some communities were looking anew at their long-defunct laws allowing Bible reading in the classroom, for example. Actually, Smith concluded, *McCollum* "may be a blessing in disguise": even if it suppressed released-time classes, it would spark a new spirituality within "regular" ones.

Smith's comments neatly encapsulated the central themes of public school religious instruction after *McCollum*. Despite the dire predictions of the ruling's critics, released-time programs continued to flourish well into the 1950s. Some schools brazenly defied the Supreme Court, while others adjusted their WRE [Weekday Religious Education] systems to comply with its decision. In the end, as Smith foresaw, *McCollum* would have a greater impact on religious practices in "regular" classes than it would on released time itself. Anticipating the eventual demise of WRE, states and school districts estab-

The Supreme Court Finds Religious Education in Public Schools to Be Unconstitutional

Pupils compelled by law to go to school for secular education are released in part from their legal duty upon the condition that they attend the religious classes. This is beyond all question a utilization of the tax-established and tax-supported public school system to aid religious groups to spread their faith. And it falls squarely under the ban of the First Amendment (made applicable to the States by the Fourteenth) as we interpreted it in *Everson v. Board of Education*. There we said: Neither a state nor the Federal Government can set up a church. Neither can pass laws which aid one religion, aid all religions, or prefer one religion over another. Neither can force or influence a person to go to or to remain away from church against his will or force him to profess a belief or disbelief in any religion. No person can be punished for entertaining or professing religious beliefs or disbeliefs, for church attendance or nonattendance. No tax in any amount, large or small, can be levied to support any religious activities or institutions, whatever they may be called, or whatever form they may adopt to teach or practice religion.

McCollum v. Board of Education,
333 US 203 (1948).

lished in-school religious exercises that all of their students—at least in theory—could accept. But controversy would soon surround these so-called common-core practices, too, setting the stage for America's next great religious upheaval in the early 1960s.

Initial reactions to *McCollum* often assumed an apocalyptic tone, summoning imagery of hellfire and damnation. Critics also drew on the new red-hot rhetoric of the Cold War, condemning the decision as a victory for "Godless Communism" over American freedom. "If the Supreme Court are free to say what liberties we have every Monday morning, we are like the peasants of Russia, under their Politburo," screamed an angry resident of Illinois. Under the Court's ruling, an Oklahoma newspaper complained, schools could teach the Communist Manifesto but not the Sermon on the Mount. Others compared *McCollum*'s attack on released time to the *Dred Scott* decision of 1857, which upheld slavery: in each case, they argued, Americans could justifiably flout the Court in the name of Christ's higher law. Still other critics invoked their rights as parents. "So the U.S. Supreme Court says I can't have my kid released from school an hour a week to study religion in my church?" asked a shopkeeper in Ohio. "The Supreme Court can go jump in the lake, so far as I'm concerned."

Following this initial burst of indignation at *McCollum*, however, critics came to realize that they had vastly exaggerated both its scope and its effect. Since the decision's Illinois test case involved WRE classes inside public schools, state and local school officials quickly decided that it did not apply to off-site released-time instruction. But in-school classes also continued, because educators rarely took action against them. In a dance of mutual evasion, local school boards deemed the issue a state concern; thereafter, state superintendents declared it a local one. Four months after *McCollum* only three states had ordered a halt to in-school WRE. And they found the ban unenforceable. "There is no possible way my office can control such a situation," Michigan's education commissioner told a local church council after his department ostensibly barred released time. "There are 15 large school districts and 300 smaller school districts who teach religious education in school buildings." Enforcing this lone order would require his office to hire at least a thousand extra employees, the commissioner concluded.

To be sure, released-time enrollment declined—probably by 10 percent—in the wake of *McCollum*. Some in-school programs moved to churches and other off-site locations, creating new transportation problems; others disbanded altogether, fearful of legal challenges and increased expenses. But nationwide WRE registration soon returned to its pre-*McCollum* level, spurred by a second Supreme Court decision: *Zorach v. Clauson* (1952). Upholding New York's WRE system, *Zorach* made explicit what northern school officials had already presumed: if released time occurred outside schools and without public funds, it was constitutional. After struggling in the shadows of *McCollum* for four years, religious educators hailed *Zorach* as a ray of sunlight. "Weekday Religious Education Has a Future!" proclaimed the longtime WRE leader Erwin L. Shaver. Thanks to *Zorach*—the "Magna Carta" of WRE, as Shaver called it—released-time programs could at last operate in full confidence of their legality. A rise in registration was sure to follow, Shaver wrote, as more and more Americans raced through the Court's new "green light" on WRE. . . .

Released time was still racked by the same battles between mainline denominations and fundamentalists that had raged since the 1940s. If anything, the continued growth of evangelical churches—and the ongoing erosion of traditional denominations—intensified this struggle. Vermont churches announced a new rural WRE project in 1954 to combat the New England Fellowship [NEF], a Boston-based fundamentalist group that sent teachers into remote areas to "win all of the young people in the community for Christ." But the NEF continued to flourish, both in Vermont and in Maine: by 1960 nearly a fifth of Maine school districts reported WRE instruction by a teacher from the fellowship. Other mainline critics focused their bile on the Rural Bible Mission, which masqueraded as a denominational movement in order to gain a foothold in the public schools. "School boards frequently thought these teachers represented the regular, organized, cooperating churches," wrote an angry mainline WRE worker in Michigan, "whereas they really represented only a segment of the fundamentalist group." All the more reason to infuse the regular school curriculum with "more religious teaching," a St. Louis church council urged, which would honor Americans' shared "theistic tradition" as well as enhance their "interfaith understanding."

The final remark illustrates the most significant new development in religious education in the 1950s: the quest for a "common core" of values and practices that could bind the different faiths together. The effort began amid the initial after-shock of *McCollum*, when churchmen feared that released-time programs would crumble and die. "What we need for the public schools," proposed the WRE advocate D. Leigh Colvin in April 1948, "is to find a universal and non-sectarian moral code as a substitute for the religious instruction forbidden by the decision of the Supreme Court." Fortunately, Colvin added, America already had one: the Ten Commandments, "the recognized moral code of the nation irrespective of denominations." Back in 1916 Colvin had spearheaded an interfaith effort to print posters of the Commandments and distribute them to public schools. From Washington, D.C., to Wichita, boards of education had approved their display. Reviving this effort would provide "a successful non-sectarian substitute" for banned released-time programs, Colvin argued. So would daily readings of the Bible, which more than a dozen state courts had already deemed a "non-sectarian" book. . . .

Just like advocates of released time, supporters of religious instruction in the "regular" curriculum often championed it as a weapon against the Red menace. "In these days of worldwide conflict between the free world and the slave world of godless communism, it is more vital than ever before that our children grow up with a sense of reverence and dedication to Almighty God," proclaimed Governor Thomas E. Dewey of

New York, praising his state's Regents' prayer. In Ohio a proponent of in-school Bible reading warned that American "subversives" typically lacked "religious conviction"; the more students learned about scripture, by implication, the less they would listen to radical appeals. "Why is there such a deep and renewed concern today about religion in the public schools?" asked an educator from Spokane, Washington, kicking off a discussion on the subject at a conference in 1955. The audience quickly agreed on an answer: "Fear of the materialistic philosophy of communism." To prevail in its global struggle, speakers argued, America would have to rediscover the "theistic tradition" that had formerly united it.

At the same conference, however, other participants urged "that theism not be perverted into humanistic ritualism"— that is, into a set of superficial bromides, "uniting" all religions but satisfying none of them. Their worries pointed to deep divisions among Americans over so-called common religious practices in the schools, which sparked just as much controversy as WRE programs did. Fundamentalists expressed the sharpest concerns, welcoming schools' renewed emphasis on the Bible and prayer but blasting their effort to combine— or, worse, to equate—different faiths. "With the Jews, Roman Catholics, Mormons, and other religious interests . . . Jesus Christ as the Messiah and Saviour of men could not be taught," fumed a Philadelphia fundamentalist group, attacking a proposed program on "shared" beliefs in the city's public schools. "Any religion that is worthy of the name must present the way of everlasting life." Despite its nonsectarian pretense, the fundamentalists added, Philadelphia's "common-core" project was "nothing more than the 'sectarian' program of the ecumenical movement."

In a classic case of strange bedfellows, Jews frequently joined fundamentalist Christians in rejecting the common-core approach. "If faith in God is to be inculcated in the schools in such a manner as to do no violence to the beliefs of

Catholic, Protestant, and Jew, it will be so pallid and anemic as to be meaningless," cautioned New York's Board of Rabbis in a near-perfect echo of the fundamentalist position. Another New Yorker worried that schools were actually evolving "a strange new hybrid religion," as distasteful to Jews as it was to other faiths. More typically, Jews charged that this supposedly common religion was simply a subterfuge for smuggling Christianity into the classroom. Under the guise of "shared" beliefs, for example, Kansas kindergartners sang a hymn about Jesus' love; a Massachusetts junior high school showed the Nativity movie *Three Wise Men*; an Indiana principal donned clerical robes to lead a high school Good Friday service; and in an Easter assembly in Florida students reenacted the Crucifixion. However much school policies might stress America's "common" faith, a Pittsburgh Jewish leader told local educators, Christian teachers would inevitably twist religious instruction toward their own distinctive beliefs.

"[I]ntense cultural conflict ultimately leads to the breakup of the country into the 'Regional States of North America' after a 'short and relatively bloodless' civil war."

Conservative Catholic Organization Opus Dei Thrives on Culture War

Rob Boston

Rob Boston is an author and activist for strict separation of Church and State. He is the author of the book Close Encounters with the Religious Right: Journeys into the Twilight Zone of Religion and Politics. *In this viewpoint, he portrays the conservative Roman Catholic group Opus Dei as a secretive society that works to influence government by recruiting powerful members. He notes that the group doesn't shy away from the Culture War, with one of its leaders—Father C. John McCloskey III— writing of the possibility of a full-scale civil war over the culture.*

As you read, consider the following questions:

1. What does the Latin phrase "opus dei" translate to in English?

2. For Catholics, how does church-going correlate to likelihood of being a member of the Republican party?

3. According to Opus Dei operative Father C. John McCloskey's futuristic vision, how would the breakup of the United States help conservative Christians?

Opus Dei, Latin for "work of God," has, according to media reports, at least 3,000 members in the United States but its influence, critics say, has been more substantial than its numbers would indicate. In 2002, an Opus Dei priest, the Rev. C. John McCloskey III, former director of the Catholic Information Center, converted [United States Senator] Sam Brownback [Republican from Kansas] from evangelical Protestantism to Catholicism. Brownback's conversion was shepherded by [United States Senator] Rick Santorum [Republican from Pennsylvania], a conservative Catholic and Opus Dei booster.

Long the scourge of progressive Catholics, Opus Dei, with an estimated 80,000 members worldwide, has enjoyed a close relationship with the church's conservative hierarchy, serving, as one writer put it in the mid 1980s, as a "holy mafia" to promote far-right views on "culture war" issues.

The organization has long had its own order of priests, and in 1982, Pope John Paul II granted Opus Dei special status known as a "personal prelature." That means the group is overseen by its own bishop, who reports directly to the pope. Opus Dei is the only organization to enjoy such unique privileges.

For many years, Opus Dei remained secretive and mysterious. Rumors swirled that some members engaged in strange rituals, such as "mortification of the flesh" by wearing a cilice, a small, spiked chain worn around the thigh that pricks the skin. The group was accused of targeting impressionable college students and restricting their access to family members. Some critics labeled Opus Dei a cult.

Although these charges frequently resurface, it's the group's ties to reactionary politics and ultra-orthodox forms of Catholicism that generate most interest these days. Under the conservative papacy of John Paul II and his successor, Benedict XVI, Opus Dei is seen as an increasingly powerful organization dedicated to fending off liberalism in the church and advancing a hard-right political agenda. . . .

Recruiting the Rich and Powerful

Opus Dei does not publish a directory of members but is known for its interest in targeting the rich and powerful. Over the years, rumors have surfaced that certain high-profile Catholics might be members. Supreme Court Justices Antonin Scalia and Samuel A. Alito have been fingered as possibilities. There is no proof in either case, but *Newsweek* magazine reported in 2001 that Scalia's wife has attended functions at the Catholic Information Center, and his son Paul, a Catholic priest, has spoken there.

Santorum is also pegged as a possible member. In 2002, Santorum attended an Opus Dei event in Rome, during which he attacked President John F. Kennedy's famous 1960 endorsement of church-state separation. Santorum said the Kennedy vow not to enforce Catholic doctrine through civil law has caused "much harm in America" and went on to describe President George W. Bush, a Methodist, as the nation's first true Catholic president.

"From economic issues focusing on the poor and social justice, to issues of human life, George Bush is there," Santorum told the *National Catholic Reporter*. "He has every right to say, 'I'm where you are if you're a believing Catholic.'" . . .

Attacking Liberal Catholics

Opus Dei's Washington operative McCloskey is certainly no fan of progressive movements within Catholicism. He once opined, "A liberal Catholic is oxymoronic. The definition of a

Opus Dei's Opponents Are Jealous of Its Success

Opus Dei is a predominantly lay movement (the number of priests, about two thousand, is kept at a certain ratio to nonclerical members) dedicated to sanctifying people's lives in the midst of their everyday work and responsibilities. That used to be the cry of the progressives themselves. Now that someone has actually succeeded at it—albeit without accepting the progressive religious and social ideology lay movements were supposed to bring with them—the progressives themselves speak darkly of a parallel church that bypasses the local bishops (a false charge), of cult-like brainwashing of young people (to judge by the young people in Opus Dei centers here in America, equally false), and of a sinister right-wing political and economic conspiracy global in its reach (if true, a miserable failure given the current dearth of right-wing regimes on every continent).

Robert Royal, "Opus Dei," First Things, May 1998.

person who disagrees with what the Catholic Church is teaching is called a Protestant."

McCloskey, who is now a research fellow at the Faith & Reason Institute for the Study of Religion and Culture in Washington, D.C., spends a good deal of his time penning columns lamenting secular government and opposing dissent from church teachings.

Bemoaning the decline of Christianity in Europe in a 2005 column, McCloskey wrote, "Here in America, the increasing chasm between alternative worldviews evidenced by the election of November 2000 and the bitter battles over the confirmation of federal judges shows our need to learn from Europe's lesson. Whatever the outcome, the United States is at most only decades away from taking a decisive turn one way or another, either becoming a largely Christian nation, in keeping with our origins, or following Europe into a radical secularism on its way to obsolescence, overwhelmed by demographic shrinking and immigration."

Voting Republican

In a May 2004 column, McCloskey wrote, "As the sole remaining world power today, America's influence is enormous, for good or evil. I believe that either America will become a largely Catholic country in the course of this century or America may well cease to be (at least in the form we now know). . . ."

McCloskey also celebrates the trend of church-going Catholics to closely identify with the GOP [the Grand Old Party, or Republican Party]. In a column published earlier this year, he wrote, "Since the 1960s, there has been a clear shift towards the Republican party and away from the Democratic party by Catholic voters. When the polls differentiate between church-going and non-church-going Catholics, Republicans dominate by a wider margin among the church-going, and Democrats among the non-church-going.

"I would extrapolate," he continued, "that the more orthodox in belief and regular in church attendance the Catholic American, the more likely he is to vote for Republicans, whose national platform, particularly on non-negotiable matters such as abortion, homosexual marriage, and embryonic experimentation, is more in sync with the Church's teachings."

Foreseeing an Actual War

In a *Catholic World Report* essay published in 2000, McCloskey outlines a futurist fantasy with chilling religious and political implications. Supposedly written in the year 2030 by "Father Charles" (McCloskey's rarely used first name), it alludes to a brutal 21st-century persecution of the Catholic Church in America that results in "tens of thousands of martyrs." This intense cultural conflict ultimately leads to the breakup of the country into the "Regional States of North America" after a "short and relatively bloodless" civil war.

Some states "worship at the altar of the 'culture of death,'" says Father Charles, while others adopt Christianity as a governing principle. It's the red states/blue states divide carried to the ultimate extreme.

While the prospect of religious persecution and civil war may sound horrific to most Americans, McCloskey sees a bright side.

"The outcome was by no means an ideal solution," observes his fictional priest, "but it does allow Christians to live in states that recognize the natural law and divine Revelation, the right of free practice of religion, and laws on marriage, family and life that reflect the primacy of our Faith."

In the essay, McCloskey foresees a smaller Catholic Church in the future, but he predicts that it will be much more obedient and will include "hundreds of thousands of Evangelical Protestants" who convert to Catholicism. (Other faiths will be targeted for proselytism as well; "We will convert those Moslems yet," his fictional priest adds exultantly.)

Breakfast and Politics

Perhaps to help cement their bonds to the GOP, Opus Dei and other ultra-orthodox Catholic groups began sponsoring a "National Catholic Prayer Breakfast" in Washington in 2004. The annual event is essentially a feast for the Catholic right and features Republican Party operatives and elected officials. Bush spoke at the 2005 breakfast and appeared at this year's [2006] gathering as well. (McCloskey served on the board of advisors for the inaugural breakfast.)

Religion News Service reported that at the 2004 event, only one Democratic lawmaker attended and noted its heavy partisan feel, writing, "At times it seemed the only thing missing was a Republican elephant."

Influencing the Legislative Agenda

In Washington, Opus Dei relies on influential senators like Santorum and Brownback to advance its agenda. The two are known for frequently pushing "culture war" issues, including ardent opposition to abortion and gay rights and the promotion of "intelligent design" in public school science classes.

Since Brownback's conversion, he has become even more vocal on social issues. A recent *Rolling Stone* profile titled "God's Senator" notes that the Kansas Republican is co-sponsoring legislation called the Constitution Restoration Act.

Labeling the measure Brownback's "most bluntly theocratic effort," *Rolling Stone* described the bill like this: "If passed, it will strip the Supreme Court of the ability to even hear cases in which citizens protest faith-based abuses of power. Say the mayor of your town decides to declare Jesus lord and fire anyone who refuses to do so; or the principal of your local high school decides to read a fundamentalist prayer over the PA every morning; or the president declares the United States a Christian nation. Under the Constitution Restoration Act, that'll all be just fine."

> "As citizens, we're free to believe what we wish about ultimate reality, and indeed this pluralist freedom of belief is a cardinal good to be protected in liberal democracy."

State Neutrality Allows Peaceful Coexistence between the Religious and Nonbelievers

Thomas W. Clark

Thomas W. Clark is director of the Center for Naturalism. In this viewpoint, Clark explains the deeply rooted conflict between scientific and religious worldviews. Empiricism, the idea that humans can agree only on evidence from the material world, informs the scientific worldview. Religion, in contrast, entertains ideas about meaning and the ultimate purpose of life. Different religious traditions have different ideas about these things—there can be no agreement. Clark believes that the state should be neutral with regard to metaphysical questions; public policy should be based only on empirical evidence. Things that can be seen and experienced are the only proper basis for agreement between people of differing faiths.

Thomas W. Clark, "Naturalism vs. Supernaturalism: How to Survive the Culture Wars," *The Humanist*, vol. 66, no. 3, May-June 2006, pp. 20–25. Reproduced by permission of the author.

As you read, consider the following questions:

1. What are some examples of religious and/or metaphysical questions mentioned in the article?

2. What are some of the reasons Clark gives for scientific explanations appealing to people? Likewise why is faith appealing?

3. How does a heterogeneous society help promote an empirical approach to public policy?

The culture wars have, at their root, a conflict between two drastically different ways of understanding reality: one essentially empiricist, the other decidedly not. The liberal-democratic political solution to such conflict is to provide a neutral public space within which differing worldviews make their case. But the very existence of such space and our pluralist society are threatened by totalitarian ambitions for ideological conformity. This threat is best countered by promoting empiricism, not faith, as the basis for knowledge.

Irrenconcilable Differences

Central to the culture wars is the conflict between science and faith and, derivatively, between naturalism and supernaturalism. As much as some think that science and faith constitute what paleontologist Steven J. Gould called "non-overlapping magesteria," or separate, non-conflicting domains of authority, the fact remains that both make claims about the actual world, and these claims often conflict. Was the Virgin Mary's conception literally immaculate, and did Jesus literally rise from the dead? Does an immortal soul animate the newly formed embryo? Did God give us contra-causally free wills so that we—not God—bear ultimate responsibility for good and evil? Is there a "higher power" or intelligence that transcends the physical world? Are life forms designed by this intelligence, or are they the product of random mutation and natural selection? Science and faith-based religions might well have different answers to such questions.

The Law Should Be Based Strictly on Science

The law in most Western states is a public institution designed to function in a society that respects a wide range of religious and otherwise metaphysical beliefs. The law cannot function in this way if it presupposes controversial and unverifiable metaphysical facts about the nature of human action, or anything else. Thus, the law must restrict itself to the class of intersubjectively verifiable facts, i.e. the facts recognized by science, broadly construed.

Joshua Greene and Jonathan Cohen,
"For the Law, Neuroscience Changes Nothing and Everything,"
Philosophical Transactions of the Royal Society of London, *2004.*

Science and faith often disagree because they constitute dramatically different epistemologies—that is, different ways of justifying belief, ways which lead to naturalism and supernaturalism, respectively. If you're scientifically, or more broadly, empirically inclined, then you'll likely place your cognitive bet with varieties of intersubjectively available evidence. Knowledge is more or less what we can observe, or what others we trust have observed or inferred from reliable observations over the centuries. Science is the ideal of such knowledge. By means of observational evidence, inferences, and theories, science describes a single, natural world in which all phenomena are interrelated. If we take science as criterial for deciding what exists, the natural world is what is real. Absent convincing empirical evidence, you might well not believe in a god, Jesus, souls, the virgin birth, or contra-causal free will. On the other hand, if you're inclined to faith, then evidential requirements are relaxed. Based on intuition, revelation, tradition, what the Bible says, or what you're told by the local imam, you might well believe in categorically supernatural, immaterial entities. The upshot is that we have two very different takes on reality—one more or less naturalistic, the other at least partly supernaturalistic—driven by two very different epistemologies—one empiricist, the other not. (Religions that take an empirical approach to knowledge, e.g., religious naturalism, "Einsteinian religion" and the ontologically austere versions of Buddhism and Zen, won't, of course, conflict with science about the nature of reality.)

Conflicting Worldviews Are Here to Stay

So how do we as a culture handle the conflict between empiricism and non-empiricism, and the worldviews they generate? Some rather strident voices on both sides see little room for compromise. The religious right (also called the "theocratic right") routinely demonizes scientific naturalism and materialism as the devil's work, undermining the basis for meaning, morality, human freedom, and dignity. And on the secular side are militant atheists such as Richard Dawkins and Sam Harris (Pen Award-winning author of *The End of Faith*), inveighing against faith and traditional religion as (metaphorically) the devil's work, spurring narrow-minded chauvinism, ideological intolerance, and dangerous fanaticism. The hope on both sides is that the opposition will eventually dry up and blow away.

But, given that both science and faith appeal to deeply rooted human predilections, neither side is going away anytime soon. Science appeals because we are necessarily curious creatures, with insatiable appetites to understand, predict, and control our surroundings and ourselves. The discovery of how things work is intrinsically rewarding, and developing the practical applications of discoveries is no less so. On the other hand, faith appeals because, afraid of death and wanting our suffering on earth to be redeemed, we gravitate toward the possibility of having souls and gods that transcend mere matter. The desire for something beyond the natural world described by science, something that might confer ultimate purpose and significance to our lives, strongly motivates an acceptance of beliefs that have little empirical support. Someday, perhaps, we as a species will abjure this "transcendental temptation" as Humanist philosopher Paul Kurtz calls it; indeed, the decline of religious observance in Europe suggests that this is possible. But until then, the consolations of traditional faith-based religion will be integral to our culture.

The Solution: Public Neutrality and Pragmatic Empiricism

The question, then, is how to engineer a peaceful coexistence between these worldviews, one essentially naturalist, the other supernaturalist. Such coexistence wouldn't be problematic were it not for the evangelical desire, so common to the human heart, to universalize one's beliefs—what we might call the totalitarian temptation. We aren't content to have our certainties; others must share them as well, since a plurality of worldviews raises doubts about our truth. The desire for ideological conformity is sometimes expressed in attempts to coerce belief and crush opposing views, as, for instance, in the international *jihad* of extremist Islam, for which *kafirs* (infidels) are deserving of death. Secular jihads that champion decidedly unscientific, non-empirical understandings of human nature and history—racism, Nazism, the triumph of the proletariat—have been mounted as well, with horrific consequences. Were it not for fanatics who insist that we must all share their worldview or die, the problem of ideological coexistence wouldn't arise. But since they are among us, the problem is paramount.

The liberal democratic political solution to the problem of coexistence is to keep the state ideologically neutral, creating a public space of secular services and protections based in no particular cosmology or view of human nature. Within this space, differences in worldviews are debated, for the most part peacefully—and, in theory if not always in practice, the government doesn't take sides. As citizens, we're free to believe what we wish about ultimate reality, and indeed this pluralist freedom of belief is a cardinal good to be protected in liberal democracy; it's central to the individual autonomy we cherish so highly. If we are public servants, then while at work our convictions come second to the obligation to keep the public space ideologically neutral, since such neutrality is a necessary condition for everyone's freedom of conscience.

The First Amendment and Freedom of Belief

This freedom is of course explicitly codified in the First Amendment, which protects a person's right to hold the worldview (not just the religion) of her or his voluntary choice. The founders' intent, in response to harsh English colonial rule, and then the populist whims of state legislatures, was to secure an individual's freedom of conscience against the tyranny of both monarchs and majorities. Thus the separation of church and state, requiring an ideologically neutral public space, became an essential democratic precept.

This neutrality requires that when designing and justifying public policies (on issues such as abortion, civil rights, and death with dignity), the deciding arguments must refer to this world: the physical, temporal world that we all inhabit, agree exists, and know via the senses. To justify policy based on a particular view of the world to come (should it exist), without appealing to facts about the present world held in common, would necessarily marginalize other such views. It would privilege a single understanding of ultimate reality, grounded in sectarian faith or contested philosophical assumptions. This means that, whatever our worldview, we have to act as this-world empiricists when arguing for policy, citing facts potentially available to all parties to the dispute, and using shared canons of logic and evidence.

Pluralist Politics

Such pragmatic empiricism is reinforced by the realities of politics in a pluralist society. To gain support from diverse constituents, legislators have to appeal to what the electorate has in common—namely, its shared concerns about material reality, not the transcendent realm of faith, about which there is often little agreement. Trying to lock up the Christian vote by citing the New Testament might well lose you the Muslim, Jewish, atheist, agnostic, or New Age vote, so the safe bet is to steer clear of explicit religion when appealing to a heterogeneous population, and cite empirical facts instead. A diversity of worldviews, then, forces politicians to ground their arguments in the here and now, not the hereafter, which has the effect of protecting minority faiths and philosophies. Writing in the *New Republic*, Peter Beinart says,

> It's fine if religion influences your moral values. But, when you make public arguments, you have to ground them—as much as possible—in reason and evidence, things that are accessible to people of different religions, or no religion at all. Otherwise, you can't persuade other people, and they can't persuade you. In a diverse democracy, there must be a common political language, and that language can't be theological.

The burden of supplying non-sectarian, empirical justifications for policy also serves us well in a very practical sense, in that policies responsive to facts about this world are likely to be more effective than those that give faith-based claims precedence. We wouldn't, for instance, be well served in deciding environmental policy on the basis of biblically based beliefs that the End Times are near. Rather, we're better off sticking with the scientific evidence that, short of a catastrophic asteroid impact, the Earth has several millions of years ahead of it. Such public pragmatic empiricism sidesteps talk about ultimate concerns, giving us reality-based policies while avoiding conflicts between worldviews.

"We're trying to go into enemy territory ... [to] blow up the ammunition dump. What is their ammunition dump in this metaphor? It is their version of creation."

Advocates Promote a New Type of Creationism as Scientific

Barbara Forrest and Glenn Branch

Since the late 1990s, a group of scholars, led by retired law professor Phillip Johnson and mathematician William Dembski, have promoted the concept of "intelligent design"—the idea that random mutation cannot account for the apparent evolution of life on earth. Dubbed "The Wedge," this group has worked to get intelligent design taught in universities and the public schools. In this viewpoint, philosophy professor Barbara Forrest and deputy director of the National Center for Science Education Glenn Branch maintain that The Wedge is misrepresenting intelligent design as science when it is actually a tool used by religious believers in the Culture War to gain access to the classroom.

Barbara Forrest and Glenn Branch, "Wedging Creationism into the Academy," *Academe*, vol. 91 no. 1, January-February 2005, pp. 36–41. Reproduced by permission.

As you read, consider the following questions:

1. What are some of the avenues by which The Wedge promotes the acceptance of intelligent design?

2. Do most mainstream scientists endorse intelligent design? Are the scientists who do support intelligent design representative of the scientific community?

3. How have proponents of intelligent design attempted to get their ideas into the public schools?

[I]ntelligent design is the latest face of the antievolution movement, formerly dominated by "young-earth" creationists. Committed to a literal reading of the biblical book of Genesis, such creationists believe that the earth is about ten thousand years old, that species of living things were specially and separately created by God, and that speciation is possible only within biblical "kinds." Intelligent design, however, is not officially committed to such a literal reading of Genesis; in their assaults on evolution, [retired law professor Phillip] Johnson and [Mathematician William] Dembski prefer instead to invoke the mystic language of the Gospel of John: "In the beginning was the Word." Learning from the repeated failures of young-earth creationism, subscribers to intelligent design— who include a handful of young-earth creationists—seek to distance themselves from the public image of creationism as a sectarian and retrogressive pseudoscience. They thus take no official stand on the age of the earth, common descent, and the possibility of macroevolution.

Mere Creation

What they insist on is the bankruptcy of mainstream evolutionary science. The idea is to unite antievolutionists under the noncommittal banner of "mere creation" (consciously echoing popular Christian apologist C.S. Lewis's "mere Christianity"), affirming their common belief in God as creator while avoiding discussion of divisive details. They want to defer doctrinal disputes, such as those involving the age of the earth, until the public is convinced that intelligent design is a legitimate scientific alternative to evolution. Indeed, according to the Wedge's repeated announcements, intelligent design is on the cutting edge of science.[1]

Its most conspicuous feature, however, is its scientific sterility. The Wedge's most notable attempts to provide a case for intelligent design appear in books for the general reader, such as Dembski's *Intelligent Design: The Bridge Between Science and Theology* and Lehigh University biochemist Michael Behe's *Darwin's Black Box: The Biochemical Challenge to Evolution.* The few university presses (such as Cambridge and Michigan State) that have published intelligent design books classify them as philosophy, rhetoric, or public affairs, not science. There are no peer-reviewed studies supporting intelligent design in the scientific research literature. The scientific community as a whole is unimpressed and unconvinced, and intelligent design's credentials as a scientific research program appear negligible. Indeed, Dembski himself recently conceded that "the scientific research part" of intelligent design is now "lagging behind" its success in influencing popular opinion. So the Wedge needs another way to persuade education policy makers that intelligent design is academically respectable. . . .

What are the academic supporters of intelligent design doing to advance its cause? Significantly, they are not teaching it in mainstream science courses, despite Behe's declaration that it "must be ranked as one of the greatest achievements in the history of science." Access Research Network, a Wedge auxiliary, lists only two "[intelligent design] colleges": Oklahoma Baptist University (home to CSC [Center for Science and Culture] fellow Michael Newton Keas) and Biola University (formerly the Bible Institute of Los Angeles and home to CSC fellows William Lane Craig, J. P. Moreland, and John Mark Reynolds).

1. The Wedge is a name for a group of academics who promote the intelligent design viewpoint.

Americans' Attitudes toward the Evolution versus Intelligent Design Debate

Question posed: A person can believe in evolution and still believe God created humans and guided their development.

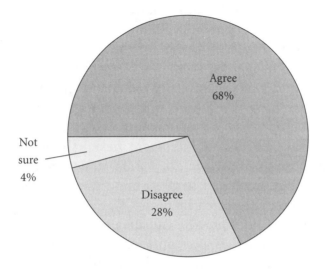

TAKEN FROM: People for the American Way, Science and Spirit Report, 2000.

On the rare occasions when intelligent design is taught as science in mainstream academia, it appears in venues not subject to the same scrutiny as regular courses: honors seminars, independent study, continuing education, not-for-credit minicourses, and interdisciplinary—especially science-and-religion—courses. Science faculty are typically not thrilled. For example, an honors course at the University of New Mexico in which intelligent design was treated respectfully was reclassified as a humanities course after the science faculty protested that students in the class were presented with material that they were not equipped to evaluate on its scientific merits, such as they were.

Conference or Congregation?

Despite the scientific sterility of intelligent design, its proponents regularly hold conferences, usually on campuses, with a view to establishing contact with sympathetic faculty and students. Early conferences, such as the Wedge's 1996 "Mere Creation" conference at Biola, were essentially "in-house" meetings of those eager to found a new antievolution movement with a broader appeal than young-earth creationism. In his introduction to the conference proceedings, published in 1998 as *Mere Creation: Science, Faith, and Intelligent Design*, Dembski describes the purpose of the conference as formulating "a theory of creation that puts Christians in the strongest possible position to defeat the common enemy of creation." He added that "mere creation is a golden opportunity for a new generation of Christian scholars." The list of contributors to *Mere Creation* is a veritable who's who of the Wedge.

The "Nature of Nature" conference, held in 2000 at Baylor under the auspices of the Polanyi Center, purported to be "an interdisciplinary conference on the role of naturalism in science." Although "naturalism" refers to a number of distinct positions in a variety of disciplines, it means only one thing to the Wedge; the enemy. (In *Mere Creation*, Dembski describes "mere creation" as "a theory of creation aimed specifically at defeating naturalism and its consequences," a definition that describes intelligent design as well.)

The Wedge lost no time in appropriating the prestige of the conference attendees (including two Nobel laureates) to advertise intelligent design and its crusade against naturalism. In *Christianity Today*, a magazine devoted to news and culture from an evangelical perspective, CSC fellow Nancy Pearcey boasted, "These scientists' willingness even to address such questions, alongside design proponents such as Alvin Plantinga and William Lane Craig, gives enormous credibility to the [intelligent design] movement." . . .

Although intelligent design conferences will probably continue to be held under such auspices on campuses across the country, recent gatherings have returned to the sectarian institutions that nurture the movement. Two major conferences—"Research and Progress in Intelligent Design" (RAPID), held in 2002, and "ID and the Future of Science," held in April 2004—were hosted by Biola, which is increasingly invested in intelligent design. Perhaps unable to find a suitable academic venue, the organizers of "Dispelling the Myth of Darwinism" held the June 2004 event at a North Carolina church; the speakers included both intelligent design stalwarts such as Behe and unreconstructed young-earth creationists such as John Morris of the Institute for Creation Research.

The Culture Wars

In his keynote address to the RAPID conference, William Dembski described intelligent design's "dual role as a constructive scientific project and as *a means for cultural renaissance*" (emphasis added). Reflecting a similar revivalist spirit, the Discovery Institute's Center for Science and Culture had been the Center for the Renewal of Science and Culture until 2002. Explaining the name change, a spokesperson for the CSC unconvincingly insisted that the old name was simply too long. Significantly, however, the change followed hard on the heels of accusations that the center's real interest was not science but reforming culture along lines favored by conservative Christians.

Such accusations appear extremely plausible, not only in the absence of any scientific research supporting intelligent design, but also in light of Phillip Johnson's claim that "Darwinian evolution is not primarily important as a scientific theory but as a culturally dominant creation story. . . . When there is radical disagreement in a commonwealth about the creation story, the stage is set for intense conflict, the kind . . . known as 'culture war.'" Similarly, the "Wedge Document" states that the goals of the Center for the Renewal of Science and Culture (as it then was) were to "defeat scientific materialism and its destructive moral, cultural, and political legacies. To replace materialistic explanations with the theistic understanding that nature and human beings are created by God."

For Johnson, the Wedge is waging a Kulturkampf [culture struggle]: "We're trying to go into enemy territory . . . [to] blow up the ammunition dump. What is their ammunition dump in this metaphor? It is their version of creation." The battlefield extends to politics, and the Discovery Institute is politically connected: its president, Bruce Chapman, held positions in the federal government during the presidency of Ronald Reagan, and U.S. Representatives John Boehner, Steve Chabot, and Mark Souder and Senators Judd Gregg and Rick Santorum have expressed sympathy for intelligent design. Indeed, Santorum proposed a symbolic "sense of the Senate" amendment to the Elementary and Secondary Education Act that tendentiously described evolution as controversial. . . .

Battle for the Public Schools

The main battlefield for intelligent design's culture war, however, is the public schools. Wedge proponents are already preparing for the inevitable legal clash over the constitutionality of teaching intelligent design. In the 1987 case of *Edwards v. Aquillard*, the U.S. Supreme Court ruled that teaching "creation science" in the public schools is a form of religious advocacy and is thus prohibited by the Establishment Clause of the First Amendment. Wedge advocates therefore strive to distinguish intelligent design from creationism in the hope that it will survive constitutional scrutiny. The fact that three members of the Supreme Court—[the late] Chief Justice William Rehnquist and Associate Justices Antonin Scalia and Clarence Thomas—have expressed dissatisfaction with the Edwards decision is doubtless a source of encouragement.

Meanwhile, despite token concessions by Dembski and Johnson that intelligent design should prove its worth to the scientific community before it enters science classrooms in public schools, and despite the professed qualms of a few intelligent design advocates, there is steady activity aimed at introducing the concept into the public school science curricula—or, failing that, of presenting "evidence against evolution," which is essentially the traditional creationist litany of supposed errors in mainstream science.

In disputes about teaching evolution in school districts across the country, intelligent design literature is now employed indiscriminately along with that of young-earth creationists. At the state level, intelligent design proponents have lobbied diligently to undermine the place of evolution in state science education standards. They consistently failed—until March 2004, when the Ohio Board of Education approved a creationist lesson plan for its new science curriculum. The lesson, "Critical Analysis of Evolution," written by intelligent design proponents, reflects a small but exploitable concession to creationists in the new science standards, which require students to learn how scientists "critically analyze aspects of evolutionary theory." Ohio may now become the Wedge's long-sought legal test case.

> "Where the effect of a 'teach the controversy' approach is to help both advocates and critics of evolutionary theory to have a better understanding ... the test of constitutionality can easily be met."

The Law Requires the Teaching of Critiques of Darwinism

David K. DeWolf and Seth L. Cooper

The teaching of Darwin's theory of the evolution of life is a major issue in the culture war. In this viewpoint, two scholars associated with the pro-intelligent design think-tank Discovery Institute—David K. DeWolf and Seth L. Cooper—review recent court decisions concerning critiques of Darwinian evolution. The authors believe the courts have decided that critiques of evolution can be taught along with Darwin's theory. In addition, they believe teachers' academic freedoms, as defined by the courts, give them the right to teach alternative theories such as intelligent design, which maintains that random processes cannot account for the complexity of life on Earth.

David K. DeWolf and Seth L. Cooper, "Teaching About Evolution in the Public Schools: A Short Summary of the Law," *Discovery Institute*, June 20, 2006. www.discovery.org. Reproduced by permission.

As you read, consider the following questions:

1. What does "teach the controversy" mean? How does the concept apply to the teaching of ideas about the origins of life?
2. What Supreme Court decision gives state legislatures the right to mandate the teaching of scientific critiques of prevailing scientific theories?
3. What is the "common ground" promoted by the Discovery Institute regarding teaching about neo-Darwinian evolutionary theory? Why do they take this position?

Few educational issues have sparked such continuing controversy and debate as the teaching of evolution. In the past, the debate has been polarized between those who advocate teaching only the positive case for evolution and those who ask either to remove evolution from the curriculum or to require teaching some form of creationism alongside evolution. (By "evolution" we mean both neo-Darwinian evolutionary theory in biology and chemical evolutionary theories for the origin of the first life from non-living chemicals.) School boards have been forced to address concerns about good science education as well as conflicting claims about constitutional limitations. But in the last decade a new approach to teaching about evolution has been developed to meet the test of good science and satisfy the courts' standards of constitutionality. This new approach uses the phrase "teach the controversy." The idea is to use scientific disagreements over evolution to help students learn more about evolution, and about how science deals with controversy. According to this approach, students should learn the scientific case for evolution, but in doing so they should study the scientific criticisms of various aspects of evolutionary theory.

The Constitution Permits Scientific Critiques of Prevailing Scientific Theories

It is clear from U.S. Supreme Court precedents that the Constitution permits both the teaching of evolution as well as the teaching of scientific criticisms of prevailing scientific theories. Those who would like to remove evolution from the curriculum altogether have been told in no uncertain terms that the right to teach about this subject is inherent in the First Amendment. At the same time, the U.S. Supreme Court has made clear that criticism of the theory of evolution may also be a required part of the curriculum. In the case of *Edwards v. Aguillard* (1987), the Court explicitly stated: "We do not imply that a legislature could never require that scientific critiques of prevailing scientific theories be taught."

Public schools have broad discretion in developing curricula. Including more scientific information about evolutionary theory, even scientific information that raises questions about its explanatory power, can satisfy the goal of improving science education. Particularly where the effect of a "teach the controversy" approach is to help both advocates and critics of evolutionary theory to have a better understanding of the claims of evolutionary theory and its supporting evidence, the test of constitutionality can easily be met.

It is important to note that legal scholars and groups with differing views about evolution have conceded the constitutionality of presenting scientific criticisms of evolutionary theory. In 1995 a broad range of legal, religious and non-religious organizations (including the American Civil Liberties Union, Americans United for Separation of Church and State and the Anti-Defamation League) signed a statement called "Religion in the Public Schools: A Joint Statement of Current Law." The joint statement of over 30 organizations agreed that "any genuinely scientific evidence for or against any explanation of life may be taught."

A Summary of Critiques of "Neo-Darwinian" Evolutionary Theory

The modern theory of biological evolution ("neo-Darwinism") makes two big claims: (1) the primary mechanism for evolution is an unguided process of natural selection acting on random mutations; and (2) all living things are ultimately descended from a universal common ancestor. Scientists have been raising criticisms about key aspects of both claims. For example, many scientists have questioned whether the selection-mutation process that accounts for small biological changes ("microevolution") is sufficient to account for the development of fundamentally new biological features and structures ("macroevolution"). Other scientists have pointed out that mutations, which are supposed to provide the raw material for evolutionary innovations, are almost always harmful, and thus would not be preserved by natural selection in the wild. Many scientists have also questioned how Darwin's mechanism can explain the origin of animal body plans more than 500 million years ago during a huge burst in biological complexity known as the "Cambrian Explosion." It is important to note that presenting scientific criticisms of existing scientific theories is not the same thing as presenting alternative theories. One can present scientific criticisms of an existing theory (this is a standard part of science) without teaching an alternative theory (such as intelligent design).

Discovery Institute, "Kansas State Science Standards and the Discovery Institute Position on the Standards," July 23, 2006. www.discovery.org.

At the same time, school boards and administrators need to bear in mind that any presentation of a science curriculum dealing with evolutionary theory should focus on scientific evidence and theories reasonably inferable from that evidence, rather than upon claims that rest upon religious beliefs. . . .

The Constitution Prohibits the Censoring of Scientific Ideas

In *Epperson v. Arkansas* (1967), the Supreme Court stated that while shaping public school curricula is within a state's power, that power does not carry with it the right to prohibit, on pain of criminal penalty, the teaching of a scientific theory or doctrine where that prohibition is based upon reasons that violate the First Amendment. "To be sure, that case dealt with a statute prohibiting the teaching of . . . the theory or doctrine that mankind ascended or descended from a lower order of animals . . . [wrote the Court]." But the same principle could be applied to the prohibition of teaching any criticism of such a theory.

In his analysis of *Epperson*, [philosophy professor] Dr. Francis J. Beckwith stated the following: "the Court is not saying that publicly supported criticism of Darwinism (or evolution) is unconstitutional, but rather, that prohibiting academic discussion of these issues in the classroom—discussions necessary for the advancement of human knowledge—is inconsistent with the First Amendment if the prohibition has the effect of advancing sectarian religious or antireligious beliefs."

Under *Epperson*, it is unconstitutional to exclude a theory simply because it is incompatible with the religious or antireligious beliefs of a dominant group. At the same time, as noted above, curriculum must be chosen based upon the educational needs and resources available to the school board. Thus, the ideal standard for science education regarding evolutionary theory is to present both the case for mainstream evolutionary theory as well as the salient criticisms that are appropriate for the age group under consideration. Teaching students both the scientific strengths and weakness of neo-Darwinian and chemical evolutionary theories is consistent with academic freedom and avoids the problematic approach to the issue that the Court faced in *Epperson*.

Mandates for Critical Thinking about Evolutionary Theory

The No Child Left Behind Act (NCLB) requires all states to implement state-wide science standards by the 2005–06 school year. . . .

The Conference Committee Report of the No Child Left Behind Act of 2001 addressed the question of whether the implementation of state standards should result in a narrowing of science education. The Report says that where controversial topics like biological evolution exist, students should be able to "understand the full range of scientific views that exist."

Five states (Kansas, New Mexico, Pennsylvania, South Carolina, and Minnesota) have already adopted science standards that require learning about some of the scientific controversies relating to evolution. In a March 2003 letter on science curriculum under NCLB, the Acting Deputy Secretary of the U.S. Department of Education stated that "The Department . . . embraces the general principles—reflected in the [NCLB report language]—of academic freedom and inquiry into scientific views or theories." It also made clear that "The NCLB does not contain any language that requires or prohibits the teaching of any particular scientific views or theories either as part of a state's science curriculum or otherwise. . . ."

What about Intelligent Design?

In recent years a number of scientists, philosophers of science, and other scholars have developed a theory known as intelligent design. The theory of intelligent design argues that some features of the universe are best explained as the products of an intelligent cause. Many scholars working on intelligent design are affiliated with Discovery Institute, a non-profit, non-partisan think tank in Seattle, a leading advocate of the "teach the controversy" approach.

As a matter of public policy, Discovery Institute opposes any effort to mandate or require the teaching the theory of intelligent design by school districts or state boards of education. Recognizing the potential for sharp conflict in this area, Discovery Institute believes that a curriculum that aims to provide students with an understanding of the strengths and weaknesses of neo-Darwinian and chemical evolutionary theories (rather than teaching an alternative theory, such as intelligent design) represents a common ground approach that all reasonable citizens can agree on.

Beyond the question of what a school board should mandate as part of its science curriculum, there is the question of [whether] a teacher has a constitutional right to teach more than the school board requires with regard to theory of intelligent design. In December 2005, a federal trial judge in Pennsylvania made a controversial ruling that it would be unconstitutional to teach the theory of intelligent design in public school science class. However, the decision in that case, *Kitzmiller v. Dover Area School Board*, was never appealed to an appellate court. Beyond the actual parties to a lawsuit, trial opinions such as *Kitzmiller* do not have the force of law. Moreover, the decision in the *Kitzmiller* ruling was based upon evidence and characterizations of intelligent design that have been sharply contested by leading proponents of intelligent design. Accordingly, the U.S. Supreme Court's decision in *Edwards v. Aguillard* remains the federal courts' authoritative pronouncement on the teaching of scientific alternatives to evolutionary theory.

The Right to Academic Freedom

Without attempting to predict specific outcomes in specific cases that might arise in the future, a few general comments can be made. First, the U.S. Supreme Court's opinion in *Edwards v. Aguillard* contains a strong affirmation of the individual teacher's right to academic freedom. It also recognized that, while the statute requiring the teaching of creationism in that case was unconstitutional, ". . . teaching a variety of scientific theories about the origins of humankind to schoolchildren might be validly done with the clear secular intent of enhancing the effectiveness of science instruction." On the other hand, courts have recognized that teachers in K-12 public schools are subject to reasonable curricular guidelines, so long as those guidelines are applied consistently to all teachers and issues. Moreover, courts are aware of the danger that a teacher will use the classroom to advance personal religious (or anti-religious) views. As a result, science teachers should avoid even the appearance of exploiting a captive audience as distinguished from helping students develop critical thinking skills.

Periodical Bibliography

The following articles have been selected to supplement the diverse views presented in this chapter.

William Donohue	"The Real Agenda of Catholics for a Free Choice," *The Daily Catholic*, October 10, 2002.
Economist	"The Religious Left," November 11, 2004.
Riane Eisler	"Spare the Rod," *YES!*, Winter 2005. www.yes-magazine.org.
Richard Goldstein	"Cartoon Wars," *Nation*, February 21, 2005.
Diana Hess	"Should Intelligent Design Be Taught in Social Studies Courses," *Social Education*, January/February 2006.
James Hitchcock	"The Schiavo Case & the Culture Wars," *Human Life Review*, Summer 2005.
Esther Kaplan	"Onward Christian Soldiers," *Nation*, July 5, 2004.
Richard John Neuhaus	"The End of Abortion and the Meanings of 'Christian America,'" *First Things*, June/July 2001.
Frank Pastore	"The National Council of Churches Should Have Died," *Townhall.com*, March 25, 2007. www.townhall.com.
Rev. Louis P. Sheldon	"The Religious Left: Sock Puppets for Atheist George Soros?" *The Traditional Values Coalition: Church Bulletin Inserts*, February, 15, 2005, www.traditionalvalues.org.
Mark D. Tooley	"God Wants Gun Control," *Front Page Magazine*, April 18, 2007. http://frontpagemag.com.
Rev. Gerald Zandstra	"Religious Leaders and Social Activism: Prophets or Captives?" *Acton Commentary*, November 19, 2003. www.acton.org.

CHAPTER 3

Is the Culture War Going Global?

Chapter Preface

Until this decade, the culture war was largely confined to the United States, and within the United States, to disputes over domestic policies. With the terrorist attacks of September 11, 2001, and the War on Terror, the term culture war has acquired an international dimension, with commentators taking note of a culture war in Europe and of the cultural differences that play a large role in the conflict between radical Islam and the West.

In Europe, there is a growing conflict between the majority of the public, which is secular, and religious believers who form a minority in the population. European countries are small, so there is little evidence of a geographic divide (like the U.S. Red-Blue divide) which is part of the culture war in the United States. Instead, there are groups of dedicated religious believers scattered throughout various European countries. These have not yet exerted much political influence, but with a growing membership, conservative religious groups may yet become politically powerful. Much of the growth in the population of believers can be attributed to Muslim immigrants and their children. Muslims are not the only growing segment of religious conservatives. Political scientist Eric Kaufmann of Birkbeck College, University of London has pointed out that "secularization appears to be losing force in its own backyard [i.e., Europe]" as religious believers (whether they attend church or not) have more children than non-believers. These believers tend to self identify as politically conservative. Kaufmann predicts that the 15–20 percent advantage in fertility among religious believers will lead to a shift away from secularization.

The combination of an increasing proportion of homegrown religious believers and a growing conservative Muslim immigrant population is leading to a culture war that is in some ways familiar to Americans but with its own unique characteristics. In England, for example, there have been alliances between conservative Christian groups and Muslims to fight against secular liberal policies such as gay marriage and abortion. This does not mean that the conservative religious groups agree on everything. True believers are most apt to engage in religious conflict—it was after all the children of Muslim immigrants who, after rediscovering their Islamic faith, bombed the London subway system in July of 2005. Conservative columnist Mark Steyn worries that the increased Islamic presence will change Europe beyond recognition: "Europe by the end of this century will be a continent after the neutron bomb: The grand buildings will still be standing but the people who built them will be gone." Ignoring such fears, some in the Christian conservative minority have made alliances with the Muslim minority which are effectively challenging the dominance of the secular majority in countries throughout Europe.

If Kaufmann's predictions are correct, the next decades will bring increasing cultural conflict in Europe as progressive, secular populations lose ground to both Muslims and Christians. The heating up of a culture war in Europe seems likely, although it will look very different from that we have experienced in the United States. The next chapter explores how the culture war might develop outside the United States.

"Between conservative Catholics, the expanding Muslim community and growing numbers of evangelical Protestants, an alliance is being forged."

Religious Conservatives Find Common Ground in the Culture War

Cristina Odone

Christina Odone is a British writer who specializes in religious issues. She is the author of A Perfect Wife. *In this viewpoint, Odone describes the politicization of religious conservatives in Europe. While this phenomenon has been going on in the United States for more than two decades, it is relatively new on the other side of the Atlantic. Distinctly European is the importance of Muslims, who make up a larger percentage of the European population than in the United States. Odone's article highlights interfaith alliances between conservative Catholics, Muslims, and Evangelical Christians, all of whom are opposed to "secularist" policies such as gay marriage and abortion on demand.*

As you read, consider the following questions:

1. How is politicization of religion in Britain and Europe similar to the same politicization in the United States? How is it different?

2. What are some examples from the article of people of differing faiths actually working together?

3. Does Odone present any evidence of fundamentalist Christians and Muslims working together on policy issues? Do you believe such cooperation is likely to become commonplace?

Moral majority politics, which helped sweep Bush to victory, are coming here [Europe]. Muslims, conservative Catholics and evangelicals want to change Britain.

Religious Conservatism Grows in Europe

The schoolgirl talks eloquently about how she attends the Christian Union at her school, doesn't believe it is "right" to have sex before marriage, and regards the family unit as a sacred ideal. Is this teenager a hick who attends a creationist school in the Kansas plains? No, she is a middle-class, metropolitan student at St Paul's Girls' School in west London—for generations the top choice of the fee-paying chattering classes.

The young Muslim man sits in the canteen at work and confides that he is not going to continue voting for Labour politicians who allow the media to show sex and violence on the telly and his teenage daughter to get the morning-after pill over the counter, but won't allow her to wear a veil because it conflicts with her school uniform. This Muslim is not sitting in the backstreets of Beirut. He works for the BBC and lives in north London.

In the aftermath of the US elections, the chattering classes in Britain have portrayed the moral majority in America as the peculiar aberration of a raw, uncivilised culture. The religious right that swept George W Bush to victory is, they insist, a phenomenon that doesn't travel beyond American shores.

Wrong. It's an important presence here already, as is the Muslim conservatism that Asian and Arab communities have been slowly but surely unpacking in Europe, and in Britain in particular.

Religion Is Being Politicized on Both Sides of the Atlantic

A week before Americans re-elected their God-fearing president, the president of the European Commission was forced to withdraw his entire team of commissioners when Rocco Buttiglione, a Catholic candidate, condemned homosexuality as sinful and single mothers as "a bad thing". On the same day as the US election, a Muslim with dual Moroccan/Dutch nationality killed the Dutch film-maker Theo van Gogh for having made a "blasphemous" film about women and Islam. And Peter Vardy, a Christian evangelical entrepreneur, last month lost a battle to take over a school in Doncaster and turn it into a city academy that would tell children that creationism—the belief that God literally created the world in six days—is a theory on a par with Darwinism.

The politicization of religious groups that has taken place across the Atlantic and been given impetus by the presidency of the born-again Bush may not yet find a direct parallel here; Europe offers no equivalent to the Christian right in terms of numbers of votes, or influence. Yet between conservative Catholics, the expanding Muslim community and growing numbers of evangelical Protestants, an alliance is being forged. Its aim is to protect a faith-based value system against the encroaching secularism of the west. The difficulty is that, just as the religious right believe wholeheartedly that theirs is the one true way, secularists are adamant about their beliefs and intolerant of those who do not share them. The ensuing clash of

Evangelicals Revive Christianity in Europe

Evangelical churches are growing in Europe with most of their new membership being immigrants from Asia and Africa.

This growth comes at a time when the traditional European churches are shrinking. . . . While only about 2 percent of the population belong to evangelical churches, they are also influencing the practices of protestant denominations and the Catholic Church. "Non-belief, doubt and secularization continue to progress, but increasingly we're witnessing a spiritual turning in recent years," said Christopher Sinclair of the University of Strasbourg. "What's striking about the evangelical movement is that it's growing. You can see this throughout Europe. It's answering a spiritual need." Unlike evangelicals in the United States, those in Europe have stayed outside politics. "We evangelicals in France are a minority among a Protestant minority," said Etienne Lhermenault, general secretary of the Federation of Evangelical Baptist Churches of France. "So we have a minority mentality. Our American evangelical friends have a majority mentality, even if they're not exactly the majority."

"Evangelicals Revive Christianity in Europe," UPI NewsTrack, *November 18, 2006. Reproduced by permission.*

cultures will spill over into the political arena and change government policies forever.

In a post-communist world, where the market is accepted by all, conventional political divisions over taxes, government spending and big business are giving way to more deeply felt differences on issues such as when life begins, the make-up of the family unit and the boundaries of medical science. Adrian Woolridge, US correspondent of the *Economist* and co-author of *The Right Nation*, sees Britain progressing from the class politics of the trade unions, through the managerial politics of the Blair-Brown era, "to arguments about the sort of people we are and what we value. Profound issues, in short, are coming back to the centre stage of politics."

Fed up with Secular Culture

Such issues, touching on questions of identity and allegiance, generate feverish emotions. The row over Buttiglione was furious and claimed the professional scalps of two proposed commissioners; the row over Theo van Gogh's film on Islam claimed his life. Although very few moral conservatives would sanction murder (even in America, with its killings of abortionists, such events are rare), they feel that their anger is warranted. They have witnessed what they see as the liberal elite allow abortion at 28 weeks and permit the sale of the morning-after pill over the counter; they have listened to plans to legalise gay marriage and euthanasia.

In their view, the pervasiveness of the west's secularist fervour goes beyond legislation. The moral traditionalists have watched every marketing outlet from television to billboards push their children into a precocious sexualisation; they have heard of endless books, magazines and lifestyle gurus instructing their women to go out and work and establish themselves as equal to men. And they have listened to councillors and local authorities tell them that Christmas cannot be celebrated as a holy holiday in public institutions, and that their daughters may not wear the *hijab* at school.

They've had enough.

A Coalition of People of Faith

They want, now, to voice their grievances and redress perceived wrongs by voting out godless politicians and voting in representatives who will draft and change policies in accordance with their traditionalist values. In this campaign, Muslims and Christians—in particular the increasing number of born-again evangelicals—have found common cause.

"There is an informal coalition between people of faith and people who are looking for some kind of value framework," agrees the Bishop of Leicester, Tim Stevens. "People of different faiths can coalesce around a number of freedoms which we believe make for human flourishing. We can coalesce around the notion of freedom from poverty, fear, injustice—and, too, from consumerism. We are looking for some way of assigning value to human beings that is more than their place in the market."

In Warwickshire, Nuala Scarisbrick, administrator of Life, the anti-abortion charity, finds "a marked sea change in the past few years. Our volunteers and paid staff, once predominantly Christian, are today members of every religious group, from Islam to Hinduism and even Buddhism. They believe, just as Christians do, that one of the fundamental principles in their ethics is the right to life, and are prepared to fight for the right of the unborn."

Inayat Bunglawala, spokesman for the Muslim Council of Britain, agrees: "More devout Muslims will want to see the government take a stronger line on abortion—rather than as things are right now, which leave it to the individual MP's conscience. Similarly with gay marriages. Even mainstream Muslims draw a line at gay marriages. They want government to support the family unit."

A "pro-life" stance is a litmus test for religious conservatives; abortion is also the issue that gave them their first important victory, with the limit at which a legal abortion can be obtained being reduced from 28 weeks to 24. Indeed, following the publication this summer of photographs of a 12-week foetus, many politicians, including Lord Steel, who drafted the original abortion law, were moved to talk of further reducing the limit for a legal abortion.

A New Clash of Cultures

Secularists, worried about such hints of religious retrenchment, are determined to hit back. They have, argues Richard Appignanesi, author of *Introducing Existentialism*, "found a fundamentalism of their own—political correctness". From banning religious messages on Christmas cards through talking of partners instead of spouses and then, more recently, calling for St Mary Magdalene school in Islington to change its name, which was deemed "divisive" in a multicultural society, the "thought police" have produced what Appignanesi calls "the slamming door of the liberal mind". Secularists, he believes, show as much of an interest in indoctrination as the religious groups they hate so much.

The liberal chattering classes find themselves at loggerheads with an ever more self-confident and vociferous constituency today. Following 11 September 2001 and the introduction in the UK of anti-terrorism legislation regarded as targeting their community, British Muslims have become far more conscious of their rights and far more vocal about their demands. "The first real clash of cultures between Muslims and the liberal secular values took place with the Rushdie affair," says Ziauddin Sardar, the Muslim commentator and author of *Desperately Seeking Paradise*. "That saw Muslims becoming vocal. Then after 11 September they became more assertive as well. They began seeking and winning access to the corridors of power, they managed to get the proposed Religious Discrimination Act on the government agenda; and the Muslim Council of Britain sent a delegation of two to deal with Kenneth Bigley's kidnappers in Iraq."

Growth in Fundamentalist Christianity

Meanwhile, some of the Christian churches are showing evidence of similar assertiveness. While the traditional Anglican and Roman Catholic churches are losing members among both laity and clergy, the growth in evangelical congregations has become phenomenal. Many attribute this popularity to the Alpha course, a ten-week, 15-session, back-to-basics introduction to Christianity. The course, according to the London-based agency Christian Research, has been taken by 1.6 million Britons. Its success (since it was founded in the UK 23 years ago, the course has produced offshoots in more than 150 countries) has kept the coffers filled and the propaganda machine churning.

Earlier this year, 1,500 billboards, 3,000 buses and 290 taxi tip-up seats across the country sported a text message: "IS there more to life than this?" alongside the words "The Alpha Course: explore the meaning of life". Alpha's basic principles are simple—faith in God, Jesus and the Holy Spirit, and a life ruled by the Bible. This black-and-white code includes no to abortion, no to sex outside marriage, and no to gay sex ever. (Gay people need to be healed, teaches Nicky Gumbel, Alpha's leading light.)

Alpha also engages members in what can only be described as exercises in self-affirmation—endlessly repeated choruses about how they have been chosen by the Holy Spirit, and how theirs is the Only True Way.

This assertiveness training has produced a batch of graduates who burn to spread the word. Given that most Alpha recruits come from the professional middle classes, their missionary zeal should be taken seriously: these lawyers, bankers and businessmen have the wherewithal to politicise their personal faith.

Religious Values Influence Mainstream Politicians

In Tony Blair, Britain has elected its most religiously devout prime minister since William Gladstone. In a foreword to a book about Labour Christians, he wrote: "Religious beliefs and political beliefs will achieve nothing until people are prepared to act on those beliefs." The Prime Minister's close personal relationship with God has come up repeatedly, most recently in his supposed conversion to Catholicism; it has also spilled into his politics.

Under Blair's stewardship, new Labour stealthily and successfully claimed territory that had traditionally been Conservative. With words such as "good" and "bad" seeping into speeches, with talk of moral responsibility and educational ethos, new Labour stole the high horse from right under the Tories. It could well prove a shrewd move: Thomas Frank, one of America's most acute observers, warns that the 21st century will be a time when "good wages, fair play, the fate of a trade union—all these are distant seconds to evolution, abortion, gay marriage".

Armed with the conviction that their value system stems from a transcendental authority, people of faith have set to work to transform our society. Their crusade against the moral bankruptcy of western Europe may soon shift from being a rallying cry to become government policy.

> "Many of Europe's national and trans-national leaders are surrendering core aspects of sovereignty and turning Europe's native populations into second- and third-class citizens in their own countries."

Secularism and Islam Challenge Traditional Christian Culture in Europe

George Weigel

Europe is facing a decline in population due to low birthrates. It is also rapidly changing its traditional social and political structures. The European Union, made up of most countries in Western Europe and some new Eastern European members, has replaced national governments in some areas of law. Attitudes on questions of morality are becoming more progressive, at least among Western European elites. George Weigel, an ethics and public policy scholar, sees a connection between this new political and social order and the rapid rise of Islamic violence among Muslim populations in Europe, themselves largely new to the continent.

As you read, consider the following questions:

1. Who does Weigel believe are the aggressors in "Culture War A"? In "Culture War B"?

2. How are Weigel's two culture wars linked?

3. What are some examples of European governments giving in to Muslim activists' demands?

Earlier this year, five days short of the second anniversary of the Madrid bombings,[1] . . . [Spanish Prime Minister Luis] Zapatero['s] government, which had already legalized marriage between and adoption by same-sex partners and sought to restrict religious education in Spanish schools, announced that the words "father" and "mother" would no longer appear on Spanish birth certificates. Rather, according to the government's official bulletin, "the expression 'father' will be replaced by 'Progenitor A,' and 'mother' will be replaced by 'Progenitor B.'" As the chief of the National Civil Registry explained to the Madrid daily *ABC*, the change would simply bring Spain's birth certificates into line with Spain's legislation on marriage and adoption. More acutely, the Irish commentator David Quinn saw in the new regulations "the withdrawal of the state's recognition of the role of mothers and fathers and the extinction of biology and nature."

The Two Culture Wars

At first blush, the Madrid bombings and the Newspeak of "Progenitor A" and "Progenitor B" might seem connected only by the vagaries of electoral politics: the bombings, aggravating public opinion against a conservative government, led to the installation of a leftist prime minister, who then proceeded to do many of the things that aggressively secularizing governments in Spain have tried to do in the past. In fact, however, the nexus is more complex than that. For the events of the

1. On March 11, 2004, al Qaeda terrorists exploded ten bombs on Madrid trains, killing nearly 200 people.

past two years in Spain are a microcosm of the two interrelated culture wars that beset Western Europe today.

The first of these wars—let us, following the example of Spain's birth certificates, call it "Culture War A"—is a sharper form of the red state/blue state divide in America: war between the postmodern forces of moral relativism and the defenders of traditional moral conviction. The second—"Culture War B"—is the struggle to define the nature of civil society, the meaning of tolerance and pluralism, and the limits of multiculturalism in an aging Europe whose below-replacement-level fertility rates have opened the door to rapidly growing and assertive Muslim populations.

The aggressors in Culture War A are radical secularists, motivated by what the legal scholar Joseph Weiler has dubbed "Christophobia." They aim to eliminate the vestiges of Europe's Judeo-Christian culture from a post-Christian European Union by demanding same-sex marriage in the name of equality, by restricting free speech in the name of civility, and by abrogating core aspects of religious freedom in the name of tolerance. The aggressors in Culture War B are radical and jihadist Muslims who detest the West, who are determined to impose Islamic taboos on Western societies by violent protest and other forms of coercion if necessary, and who see such operations as the first stage toward the Islamification of Europe—or, in the case of what they often refer to as al-Andalus, the restoration of the right order of things, temporarily reversed in 1492 by [Spanish monarchs] Ferdinand and Isabella.

The question Europe must face, but which much of Europe seems reluctant to face, is whether the aggressors in Culture War A have not made it exceptionally difficult for the forces of true tolerance and authentic civil society to prevail in Culture War B. . . .

Marginalizing Traditional Morality

In part . . . Culture War A represents a determined effort on the part of secularists, using both national and EU regulatory machinery, to marginalize the public presence and impact of Europe's dwindling numbers of practicing Christians. Relatedly, it also involves crucial questions about the beginning and end of life, nowhere more sharply posed than in the no-longer-tradition-bound Low Countries. The Netherlands has long enjoyed a reputation for legalized libertinism involving drugs and prostitution, while also leading Europe along the path to euthanasia and same-sex marriage. Now, the formerly stolid Belgians seem determined to catch up. In addition to matching their Dutch neighbors' embrace of same-sex marriage and euthanasia—half the infant deaths in Flanders in 1999–2000 were from euthanasia—the socialist/liberal coalition governing the country recently adopted legislation permitting rent-a-uterus procreation. As the Italian philosopher and government minister Rocco Buttiglione has put it, "Once, we used to quote Karl Marx when protesting against the 'alienation,' 'objectification,' and 'commercialization' of human life. Can it be possible that, today, the Left is inscribing on its banners precisely the right to commercialize human beings"—and all in the name of tolerance and equality?

Restricting Speech

Culture War A finds expression as well in efforts to coerce and impose behaviors deemed progressive, compassionate, nonjudgmental, or politically correct in extreme feminist or multiculturalist terms. In recent years, this has typically taken the form of EU member-states legally regulating, and thus restricting, public speech. Morally critical comments about homosexual behavior, for example, have been deemed "hate speech," and a French parliamentarian was fined for saying that heterosexuality is morally superior to homosexuality. . . .

This creeping authoritarianism was also evident in a January 2006 resolution of the European Parliament condemning as "homophobic" those states which do not recognize same-sex marriage and referring to religious freedom as a "source of

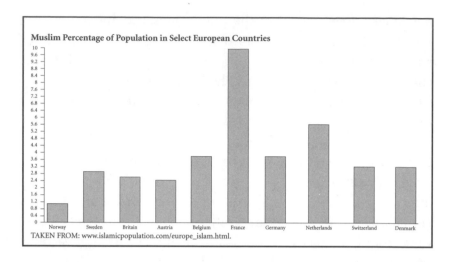

Muslim Percentage of Population in Select European Countries

TAKEN FROM: www.islamicpopulation.com/europe_islam.html.

discrimination." During the debate on that resolution, a British Euro-MP, equating traditional marriage laws with a "breach [of] the human rights of gay and lesbian people," raised the specter of the suspension of EU membership against dissenting countries like Poland and Lithuania. Poland was also threatened with a suspension of its voting rights in the EU's ministerial meetings if it were to reinstitute capital punishment.

Demographic Decline

Whatever else might be said about these developments, that Europe should find itself, at this particular moment in its history, embroiled in a sharp-edged conflict over the legal imposition of political correctness must strike even the friendliest observer as a bizarre distraction from the most dramatic fact about the continent in the early 21st century: Europe is committing demographic suicide, and has been doing so for some time. . . .

The overall picture is sobering enough. Not a single EU member has a replacement-level fertility rate, i.e., the 2.1 children per woman needed to maintain a stable population. Moreover, eleven EU countries—including Germany, Austria, Italy, Hungary, and all three Baltic states—display negative natural increase (i.e., more annual deaths than births), a clear step down into a demographic death-spiral. . . .

Over the next quarter-century, the number of workers in Europe will decline by 7 percent while the number of over-sixty-fives will increase by 50 percent, trends that will create intolerable fiscal difficulties for the welfare state across the continent. The resulting inter-generational strains will place great pressures on national politics, and those pressures may, in a variety of ways, put paid to the project of "Europe" as it has been envisioned ever since the European Coal and Steel Community, the institutional forerunner of today's European Union, was established in 1952. Demography is destiny, and Europe's demographics of decline—which are unparalleled in human history absent wars, plagues, and natural catastrophes—are creating enormous and unavoidable problems.

The Transformation of Europe

Even more ominously, Europe's demographic free-fall is the link between Culture War A and Culture War B.

History abhors vacuums, and the demographic vacuum created by Europe's self destructive fertility rates has, for several generations now, been filled by a large-scale immigration from throughout the Islamic world. For anyone who has taken the trouble to look, the most obvious effects of that immigration have been on display in continental Europe's increasingly segregated urban landscape, in which an impoverished Muslim suburban periphery typically surrounds an affluent European urban core.

Far more has changed than the physical appearance of European metropolitan areas, though. There are dozens of "ungovernable" areas in France: Muslim-dominated suburbs, mainly, where the writ of French law does not run and into which the French police do not go. Similar extraterritorial enclaves, in which *shari'a* law is enforced by local Muslim clerics, can be found in other European countries. Moreover, as Bruce

Bawer details in a new book, *While Europe Slept*, European authorities pay little or no attention to practices among their Muslim populations that range from the physically cruel (female circumcision) through the morally cruel (arranged and forced marriages) to the socially disruptive (remanding Muslim children back to radical madrassas in the Middle East, North Africa, and Pakistan for their primary and secondary education) and the illegal ("honor" killings in cases of adultery and rape—the rape victim being the one killed).

Indeed, it is not simply a case of European governments choosing to avert their gaze from such things. Europe's welfare systems generously support immigrants who despise their host countries or turn violently against them—most notably, in the London Underground and bus bombings of July 7, 2005. . . .

European Appeasement

Sixty years after the end of World War II, the European instinct for appeasement is alive and well. French public swimming pools have been segregated by sex because of Muslim protests. "Piglet" mugs have disappeared from certain British retailers after Muslim complaints that the A. A. Milne character was offensive to Islamic sensibilities. So have Burger King chocolate ice-cream swirls, which reminded some Muslims of Arabic script from the Qur'an. [Author Bruce] Bawer reports that the British Red Cross banished Christmas trees and nativity scenes from its charity stores for fear of offending Muslims. For similar reasons, the Dutch police in the wake of the van Gogh murder destroyed a piece of Amsterdam street art that proclaimed "Thou shalt not kill"[2]; schoolchildren were forbidden to display Dutch flags on their backpacks because immigrants might think them "provocative."

The European media frequently censor themselves in matters relating to domestic Islamic radicalism and crimes committed by Muslims, and, with rare exceptions, their coverage

2. Filmmaker Theodor van Gogh was killed by an Islamic extremist.

of the war against terrorism makes the American mainstream media look balanced. When domestic problems related to Muslim immigrants do come to light, the typical European re-action, according to Bawer, is usually one of self-critique. In Malmo, Sweden, the country's third-largest city, rapes, robber-ies, school-burnings, "honor" killings, and anti-Semitic agita-tion got so out of hand that large numbers of native Swedes reportedly moved out; the government blamed Malmo's prob-lems instead on Swedish racism, and chastised those who had wrongly conceived of integration in "two hierarchically or-dered categories, a 'we' who shall integrate and a 'they' who shall be integrated."

These patterns of sedition and appeasement finally came to global attention earlier this year in the Danish-cartoons *ji-had*. The cartoons themselves, depicting Muhammad, caused little comment in Denmark or anywhere else when they were originally published last year in the Copenhagen daily *Jyllands-Posten*. But after Islamist Danish imams began agitating throughout the Middle East (aided by three additional and far more offensive cartoons of their own devising), an interna-tional furor erupted, with dozens of people killed by rioting Muslims in Europe, Africa, and Asia. As Henrik Bering put it in the *Weekly Standard*, "the Danes were suddenly the most hated people on earth, with their embassies under attack, their flag being burned, and their consciousness being raised by lec-tures on religious tolerance from Iran, Saudi Arabia, and other beacons of enlightenment."

Native Europeans as Second-Class Citizens

The response from Europe, in the main, was to intensify ap-peasement. Thus the Italian "reforms minister," Roberto Cal-deroli, was forced to resign for having worn a T-shirt featur-ing one of the offending cartoons—a "thoughtless action" that, Prime Minister Silvio Berlusconi deduced, had caused a riot outside the Italian consulate in Benghazi in which eleven people were killed. Newspapers that ran the cartoons were put under intense political pressure; some journalists faced criminal charges; websites were forced to close. The pan-European Carrefour supermarket chain, bowing to Islamist demands for a boycott of Danish goods, placed signs in its stores in both Arabic and English expressing "solidarity" with the "Islamic community" and noting, inelegantly if revealingly, "Carrefour don't carry Danish products." The Norwegian government forced the editor of a Christian publication to apologize publicly for printing the Danish cartoons; at his press conference, the hapless editor was surrounded by Norwegian cabinet ministers and imams. EU foreign minister Javier Solana groveled his way from one Arab nation to another, pleading that Europeans shared the "anguish" of Muslims "offended" by the Danish cartoons. Not to be outdone, the EU's justice minister, Franco Frattini, announced that the EU would establish a "media code" to encourage "prudence"—"prudence" being a synonym for "surrender," regardless of one's view of the artistic merits of, or the cultural sensitivity displayed by, the world's most notorious cartoons.

For all the blindness of the politicians who in the 1930's attempted to appease totalitarian aggression, they at least thought that they were thereby preserving their way of life. Bruce Bawer (following the researcher Bat Ye'or) suggests that 21st-century Europe's appeasement of Islamists amounts to a self-inflicted dhimmitude[3]: in an attempt to slow the advance of a rising Islamist tide, many of Europe's national and transnational political leaders are surrendering core aspects of sovereignty and turning Europe's native populations into second- and third-class citizens in their own countries.

---

3. Dhimmitude is the second-class status of non-believers under Islamic law.

"Modernity itself may come in for criticism even as a new appreciation for the benefits of marriage and parenting might emerge."

Population Decline May Make Conservatives Culture War Victors

Stanley Kurtz

The birthrate of all industrialized countries is below the "replacement rate"—the number of children that women need to bear on average in order to avoid population decline. This situation has reversed worries about the "Population Explosion"; some thinkers now express concern that fewer young workers will be supporting a growing population of older retirees. This viewpoint by Stanley Kurtz, a research fellow at Stanford University's Hoover Institution, shows how "pro-natalist" policies (intended to make childbearing easier for families) might lead to a society-wide shift toward cultural conservatism.

As you read, consider the following questions:

1. Why do Kurtz and others view population decline as a problem?

2. What values are endangered by the current pattern of birthrates around the globe? What is the primary measure mentioned in the article to counteract this trend?

3. How might a secular (non-religious) pro-natalist program lead to increased cultural conservatism?

On the matter of the new demography and its social consequences, the work of Ben Wattenberg holds a place of special honor. In 1987, 17 years before the publication of *Fewer*, Wattenberg wrote *The Birth Dearth*. That book was the first prominent public warning of a crisis of population decline. Yet many rejected its message. In an era when a "population explosion" was taken for granted, the message of *The Birth Dearth* flew squarely in the face of received wisdom. Subsequent events, however, have proved Wattenberg right.

Despite that vindication, Wattenberg's own views have changed somewhat. Whereas *The Birth Dearth* advocated aggressive pro-natalist [favoring population growth] policies, today Wattenberg seems to have all but given up hope that fertility rates can be substantially increased. On the one hand, he thinks it unlikely that world-wide population can maintain a course of shrinkage without end. On the other hand, he sees no viable scenario by which this presumably unsustainable trend might be reversed.

The Need for Fundamental Cultural Change

In *The Empty Cradle*, Philip Longman takes a different view. Longman believes that runaway population decline may be halted, yet he understands that this can be accomplished only by way of fundamental cultural change. The emerging demographic crisis will call a wide range of postmodern ideologies into question. Longman writes as a secular liberal looking for ways to stabilize the population short of the traditionalist, religious renewal he fears the new demography will bring in its wake.

Given the roots of population decline in the core characteristics of postmodern life, Longman understands that the endless downward spiral cannot be reversed without a major social transformation. As he puts it, "If human population does not wither away in the future, it will be because of a mutation in human culture." Longman draws parallels to the Victorian era and other periods when fears of population decline, cultural decadence, and fraying social safety nets intensified family solidarity and stigmatized abortion and birth control. Longman also notes that movements of the 1960s, such as feminism, environmentalism, and the sexual revolution, were buttressed by fears of a population explosion. Once it becomes evident that our real problem is the failure to reproduce, these movements and attitudes could weaken.

Population Decline and Fundamentalist Revival

Longman's greatest fear is a revival of fundamentalism, which he defines broadly as any movement that relies on ancient myth and legend, whether religious or not, "to oppose modern, liberal, and commercial values." Religious traditionalists tend to have large families (relatively speaking). Secular modernists do not. Longman's fear is that, over time, Western secular liberals will shrink as a portion of world population while, at home and abroad, traditionalists will flourish. To counter this, and to solve the larger demographic-economic crisis, Longman offers some very thoughtful proposals for encouraging Americans to have more children. Substantial tax relief for parents is the foundation of his plan.

Longman has thought this problem through very deeply. Yet, in some respects, his concerns seem odd and exaggerated. He lumps American evangelicals together with Nazis, racists, and Islamicists in the same supposed opposition to all things modern. This is more interesting as a specimen of liberal prejudice than as a balanced assessment of the relationship between Christianity and modernity. Moreover, the mere fact that religious conservatives have more children than secular liberals is no guarantee that those children will remain untouched by secular culture.

Still, Longman rightly sees that population decline cannot be reversed in the absence of major cultural change, and the prospects of a significant religious revival must not be dismissed. In a future shadowed by vastly disproportionate numbers of poor elderly citizen, and younger workers struggling with impossible tax burdens, the fundamental tenets of postmodern life might be called into question. Some will surely argue from a religious perspective that mankind, having discarded God's injunctions to be fruitful and multiply, is suffering the consequences.

Yet we needn't resort to disaster scenarios to see that our current demographic dilemma portends fundamental cultural change. Let us say that in the wake of the coming economic and demographic stresses, a serious secular, pro-natalist program of the type proposed by Longman were to take hold and succeed. The result might not be "fundamentalism," yet it would almost certainly involve greater cultural conservatism. Married parents tend to be more conservative, politically and culturally. Predictions of future dominance for the Democratic Party are based on the increasing demographic prominence of single women. Delayed marriage lowers fertility rates and moves the culture leftward. Reverse that trend by stimulating married parenthood, and the country grows more conservative—whether in a religious mode or not.

But can the cultural engines of postmodernity really be thrown into reverse? After all, people don't decide to have children because they think it will help society. They act on their personal desires and interests. Will women stop wanting to be professionals? Is it conceivable that birth control might become significantly less available than it is today? It certainly seems unlikely that any free Western society would substan-

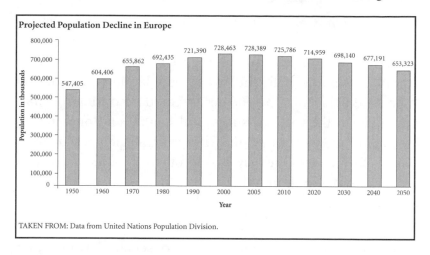

Projected Population Decline in Europe

TAKEN FROM: Data from United Nations Population Division.

tially restrict contraception, no matter how badly its population was dwindling.

Demographic Stress

Yet it is important to keep in mind that decisions about whether and when to have children may someday take place in a markedly different social environment. As mentioned, children are valued in traditional societies because of the care they provide in old age. In the developed world, by contrast, old age is substantially provisioned by personal savings and the welfare state. But what will happen if the economy and the welfare state shrink significantly? Quite possibly, people will once again begin to look to family for security in old age—and childbearing might commensurately appear more personally necessary.

If a massive cohort of elderly citizens find themselves in a chronic state of crisis, the lesson for the young will be clear. Wattenberg notes that pro-natalist policies have failed wherever they've been tried. Yet in conditions of serious economic stress and demographic imbalance, sweeping pro-natalist plans like those offered by Longman may in fact become workable. That would usher in a series of deeper cultural changes, most of them pointing society in a more conservative direction.

Then again, we may finesse the challenge of a rapidly aging society by some combination of increased productivity, entitlement reform, and delayed retirement. In that case, fertility will continue to fall, and world population will shrink at compounding speed. The end result could be crisis or change further down the road, or simply substantial and ongoing reductions in world population, with geostrategic consequences difficult to predict. One way or the other, it would seem that our social order is in motion. . . .

The Long View

Even in the celebrated image of the conservative who stands athwart history yelling "Stop!" there is a subtle admission of modernization's inevitability. [Nineteenth-century French philsopher Alexis de] Tocqueville saw history's trend toward ever greater individualism as an irresistible force. The most we could do, he thought, was to balance individualism with modern forms of religious, family, and civic association. Today, even Tocqueville's cherished counterweights to radical individualism are disappearing—particularly in the sphere of the family.

It is indeed tempting to believe that the fundamental social changes initiated in the 1960s have by now become irreversible. Widespread contraception, abortion, women in the workforce, marital decline, growing secularism and individualism—all seem here to stay. Looked at from a longer view, however, the results are not really in. We haven't yet seen the passing of even the great demographic wave of the "baby boom." The latter half of the twentieth century may someday be seen not as ushering in the end of history, but as a transition out of modernity and into a new, prolonged, and culturally novel era of population shrinkage.

The most interesting and unanticipated prospect of all would be a conservatism. . . . Longman has explored the potential ideological consequences of the new demography. In effect, Longman wrote his book to forestall a religiously-based conservatism precipitated by demographic and economic decline. Yet even Longman may underestimate the potential for conservative resurgence.

Possible Renewal in Interest in Parenting

It wouldn't take a full-scale economic meltdown, or even a relative disparity in births between fundamentalists and secularists, to change modernity's course. Chronic low-level economic stress in a rapidly aging world may be enough. There is good reason to worry about the fate of elderly boomers with fragile families, limited savings, and relatively few children to care for them. A younger generation of workers will soon feel the burden of paying for the care of this massive older generation. The nursing shortage, already acute, will undoubtedly worsen, possibly foreshadowing shortages in many other categories of workers. Real estate values could be threatened by population decline. And all these demographically tinged issues, and more, will likely become the media's daily fare.

In such an atmosphere, a new set of social values could emerge along with a fundamentally new calculation of personal interest. Modernity itself may come in for criticism even as a new appreciation for the benefits of marriage and parenting might emerge. A successful pro-natalist policy (if achieved by means of the conventional family rather than through surrogacy or artificial wombs) would only reinforce the conservative trend. In that case we will surely find that it is cultural radicals standing athwart history's new trend yelling "Stop!"

> *"The S-P's unrealistic assessment of the war on terror is dangerous, naïve, and disqualifies the secular-progressive movement from any serious participation in the post-9/11 decision-making process."*

Secular-Progressives Hinder America's Efforts in the War on Terror

Bill O'Reilly

Bill O'Reilly is the conservative creator of the television interview program The O'Reilly Factor. *In this viewpoint, O'Reilly details efforts by the American Civil Liberties Union (ACLU) to block certain government efforts in the war on terror, such as wiretapping American citizens. O'Reilly then goes on to explain the deeper roots of what he calls the "S-Ps" (for secular-progressive) viewpoint—the desire to always find fault in America. According to O'Reilly, the S-P's lack perspective; they neither recognize America's past sacrifices in global struggles nor have any idea how to devise a strategy to protect Americans from terrorists.*

As you read, consider the following questions:

1. Are the ACLU's efforts to stop wiretaps reasonable? How about their efforts on behalf of suspected terrorists held by the United States government?

2. Does O'Reilly think that eliminating global poverty is a realistic strategy in the Global War on Terror? Why or why not?

3. To what historical figure does O'Reilly compare the secular-progressives? Do you think the comparison is valid?

Who do you think Osama bin Laden supports in the American culture war: the traditionalists or the secular-progressives ["S-Ps"]?

Not so fast. . . . This may be a trick question.

On the one hand, the Saudi-born terrorist despises just about everything the S-Ps fervently espouse: a de-emphasis of religion, a libertine social landscape, no judgments on most private behavior, and an acceptance of human weakness.

For those of you not currently up to date on their policies, al-Qaeda would decapitate gays who wanted to marry, cut off the hands of drug abusers, stone to death anyone who suggested Allah not be included in the public arena, and blind anyone who looked at pornography. If Osama was calling the shots in the United States, the [American Civil Liberties Union] ACLU would be, in theory, very, very busy. In reality, they'd be dead.

But think about what I am about to put forth: From his hideout somewhere in the Muslim world, Osama bin Laden and his cohorts have got to be cheering on the S-P movement, because its most fanatical adherents are opposed to the bedrock strengths of traditional America. The S-P worldview is much softer than that of the traditional forces, as I'll demonstrate shortly. For now, it is important to understand that the S-P vanguard, the ACLU, has actively opposed just about every anti-terror strategy the U.S. government has introduced. In my view, that opposition greatly helps al-Qaeda and other terrorist outfits.

The secular-progressive movement opposes coerced interrogation—not torture, but harsh treatment—of captured terror suspects. They object to detention of them at U.S. military prisons like Guantánamo Bay [Cuba]. In addition, the ACLU opposes military tribunals (rather than civilian trials) to determine the guilt or innocence of suspected terrorists, rendition programs where terror suspects are held in foreign countries, floating wiretaps (already in use in U.S. criminal investigations), telephone surveillance of overseas calls by U.S. spy agencies, airport profiling, the Patriot Act, the war in Iraq, and random bag searches on subway or mass-transit systems.

In short, the ACLU opposes making life more difficult for terrorists but proposes absolutely nothing to make Americans safer. Osama has got to love it.

On the positive side (sarcasm intended), the ACLU supports: Constitutional protections for noncitizen terror suspects captured overseas, Geneva Convention protections for terror suspects captured wearing civilian clothing (which, of course, eliminates them from the Geneva Convention treaties), civilian lawyers and criminal due process instead of military justice, and the exposure of topsecret U.S. antiterror programs in the press.

There's more. According to the ACLU, government officials should be prosecuted for the alleged exposure of former CIA [Central Intelligence Agency] agent Valerie Plame, but at the same time no government official should be investigated for leaking information about the top-secret National Security Agency's overseas listening activities, approved by President Bush under the seal of an Executive Order.

Add it all up and you can see exactly what I meant earlier: When it comes to the war on terror, Osama bin Laden has got to be thrilled that he has unwitting allies in the ACLU and, in-

Islamic Radicals Oppose Secular Western Culture, Not Christianity

Islamic radicals like Bin Laden make their case against America and the West on the grounds that these cultures have abandoned Christianity. In his May 2006 letter to President Bush, Ahmadinejad faulted America not for being Christian, but for not being Christian enough. Many years earlier, the radical theoretician Sayyid Qutb made the same point. The main reason for the West's moral decay, Qutb argued, is that in the modern era "religious convictions are no more than a matter of antiquarian interest."

Dinesh D'Souza, "Secularism Is Not the Solution,"
Townhall.com, *February 19, 2007.*

deed, the entire S-P movement. In my assessment, the S-Ps fail to see the danger clearly. They constantly harp on America's mistakes while confronting violent terrorism, but they do not put forth viable solutions to neutralize the threats. They create a fog that damages our counterterrorism efforts. If all Americans bought into the ACLU's terror platform, instead of hiding in a Pakistani cave someplace, Osama might be sitting at a negotiating table in Paris, patiently awaiting an interview with [French newspaper] *Le Monde*.

I know I'll be harshly criticized for writing that last paragraph, but as I asked, think about it. How could any sane person adopt the stance the ACLU takes toward the war on terror? Don't those people get 9/11? Doesn't the S-P movement understand the danger America faces from terrorist fanatics who would use nuclear weapons, should they acquire them, against us?

The answer to that question is a bit complicated, but it is rooted in the one thing that the secular-progressive movement and al-Qaeda have in common: Both outfits believe that the United States of America is fundamentally a bad place.

Again, I'll be criticized for writing that, so let's back it up and return to our pal [linguist] George Lakoff, the premier S-P philosopher and guru. Like most S-P true believers, Lakoff believes that the United States is at least partially responsible for the buildup of worldwide terrorism; therefore, by that reasoning, it was some of America's own doing that it was attacked on 9/11. That point of view is obviously a tough sell to the American public, so the ACLU and others do not bring the hypothesis up very often.

But Lakoff makes the S-P position crystal clear on page 66 of his [*Don't Think of an Elephant*] book:

> The idealistic claim of the Bush administration is that they intend to wipe out all terrorism. What is not mentioned is that the United States has systematically promoted a terrorism of its own and has trained terrorists, from the contras to the mujahideen, the Honduran death squads, and the Indonesian military. Will the U.S. government stop training terrorists? Of course not. It will deny that it does so . . . if the United States wants terror to end, the United States must end its own contribution to terror.

So the war on terror is largely America's fault, according to Lakoff, who conveniently avoids mentioning America's fight against the expansion of worldwide communism. As any intelligent person knows, the brutal cold war against the Soviet Union and Red China was the primary reason the United States armed opponents of communism like the contras in Nicaragua and the mujahideen in Afghanistan.

This is so typical of Lakoff and other S-P "thinkers": They ignore all perspective in their analysis. When was the last time you heard any S-P fanatic mention that almost 3 million people were slaughtered by communist forces in Southeast

Asia after the United States withdrew from Vietnam? I've never heard Jane Fonda, a duchess of the S-P realm, mention that, have you?

The bedrock belief that America is, and has been, an evil country is crucial to understanding the secular-progressive point of view when it comes to the war on terror. Here's their bankrupt reasoning: The S-Ps cannot support any antiterror measures until the United States stops being a terrorist country itself. Get it? Yes, they're serious. If you don't believe me, travel to Berkeley, California, or Cambridge, Massachusetts, and ask.[1] . . .

A question then logically follows: How would the secular-progressives, themselves, deal with Islamic terrorism? Paging George Lakoff! He deals with that very issue on page 60 of his training manual [*Don't Think of An Elephant*]:

> Most Islamic would be martyrs not only share [fanatical religious] beliefs but have also grown up in a culture of despair; they have nothing to lose. Eliminate such poverty and you eliminate the breeding ground for terrorists . . . when the Bush administration speaks of eliminating terror, it does not appear to be talking about eliminating cultures of despair and the social conditions that lead one to want to give up his life to martyrdom.

Outstanding. Lakoff apparently believes the United States has the power to eliminate poverty and change social conditions in places like Pakistan—estimated population, 163 million. America can't even eliminate poverty and change "social conditions" in Detroit, much less Islamabad. No government can impose prosperity or benign thinking on masses of people. It is simply impossible.

But George Lakoff and the S-Ps don't care for rational analysis. It sounds so good to say that terrorism can be defeated by a change in America's foreign policy. More Lakoff:

1. Berkeley is home to the liberal University of California, likewise Cambridge is home to Harvard University.

> What is needed is a new kind of moral foreign policy, one
> that realizes that America can only be a better America if
> the world is a better world. America must become a moral
> leader using fundamental human values: caring and respon-
> sibility carried out with strength to respond to the world's
> problems.

Once again, Lakoff seems to have missed the truth of America's
great sacrifice in defeating the Soviet Union's totalitarianism
and thereby bringing freedom to tens of millions of people in
Eastern Europe and other Soviet-dominated areas. Nor does
the S-P guru mention the enormous blood and treasure
America spent defeating the Nazis and Imperial Japan. Don't
those historic achievements fall in the category of "caring and
responsibility carried out with strength to respond to the
world's problems"? Or did the United States bring World War
II upon itself as well?

It galls me that the S-Ps can get away with denigrating the
United States when it, along with Great Britain and a precious
few other countries, is standing up against a homicidal jihad
that could destroy the world.

The S-Ps' unrealistic assessment of the war on terror is
dangerous, naïve, and disqualifies the secular-progressive
movement from any serious participation in the post-9/11
decision-making process. Sure, it would be great to heal social
ills all over the world by waving a magic wand, but why bother
spouting such delusional nonsense? The S-Ps are at their best
when proposing airy theories or undermining policies with
which they disagree. They fail dismally, however, when asked
to create better, more effective policies to protect and improve
the lives of everyday people. But that failure does not deter
them; they are convinced they hold the moral high ground
and those who oppose them—their enemies in the culture
war—must be marginalized for the good of all.

And so I have arrived at this necessary conclusion: All
clear-thinking Americans *should* become opponents of the S-P

movement for the simple reason of self-preservation. If the secular-progressives ever come to power in America, and re-member, [liberal Democratic politician] Howard Dean got close, their policies would put you and your family in grave danger. Osama and his pals would love to face off against La-koff, Dean, [documentary filmmaker] Michael Moore, [finan-cier] George Soros, and the rest of the soft secular forces. In the 1930s, Adolf Hitler had a blast with Neville Chamberlain, the appeasement-supporting prime minister of Great Britain. That historical lesson might be worth revisiting in the culture war between the traditionalists and the S-Ps.

Oh, and one more thing. If you really want to see just how "caring" and humane the secular-progressive movement is, visit some of their black-hearted Web sites. If the hatred and libel you see are examples of S-P caring, somewhere the Mar-quis de Sade is cheering. One of the reasons I am writing this book is to show the great divide between how the S-Ps frame their arguments and their actual conduct. Many of these people are as ruthless as anyone you see in the Bush adminis-tration. But they hide behind the nurturing and enlighten-ment themes. To use an old Levittown expression: "What a crock."

"*People who disagree with [conservative writer William Bennett] are in turn wrong, evil, and perverse, an intellectualized/moralistic/pop-psych trifecta.*"

Conservatives Use the War on Terror to Advance Their Political Agenda

Tom De Luca and John Buell

Conservative columnist William Bennett, among others, has accused those who oppose the Iraq war and other Bush administration policies of being anti-Americans who lack the ability to discern good from evil. This viewpoint criticizes Bennett's rhetoric, showing that conservatives themselves often ignore evil when it suits their interest to do so. The authors accuse Bennett and others of using selective outrage in order to advance the conservative cause in the culture war. Political scientist Tom De Luca is the author of Two Faces of Political Apathy *and writer John Buell is the author of* Democracy by Other Means.

As you read, consider the following questions:

1. How do some conservatives such as William Bennett view those who disagree with them and/or the Bush administration in regard to the War on Terror?

2. How is Bennett being hypocritical in when he says the peace movement didn't pay attention to Saddam Hussein's crimes before the Iraq War?

3. Do the authors believe that only the conservative Right engages in demonization of its opponents?

Each of [the following intellectuals'] views plays a role in the ways the culture wars roil our nation vis-à-vis the war on terror and the invasion of Iraq. [Linguist and philosopher Noam] Chomsky is the radical critic who always seems to see the root of all problems in things the U.S. government does, yet his account is clear on bin Laden's culpability and the utter moral degeneracy of the bin Laden network. [International Law Professor Richard] Falk is the international lawyer and liberal thinker who articulates an internationalist solution that looks to the future. Yet he supported the invasion of Afghanistan, feeling that 9/11 demonstrated that current international practices and institutions are not yet up to the task of providing an adequate defense, especially in facing the stateless-actor terrorist threat. [Political theorist Jean] Elshtain articulates again her notion of the central place individual responsibility must have in our scheme of values, warns again against excusing bad or evil behavior through a cant that emphasizes prior victimization of the perpetrators of evil. Her faith in America's gifts to the world is strengthened by 9/11. The world needs both our values and us. But evil, she reminds us, can lurk in *any* heart.

A Simplistic Moral Vision

Not so with William Bennett. His post-9/11 book, *Why We Fight: Moral Clarity and the War on Terrorism*, provides few surprises, nor would he want it to. He has always had moral clarity. America and western civilization are simply superior. Israel is, too. Islam has not been hijacked. It really is intolerant in ways that cause violence. There is good and evil in the world. He is proud to be on the side of good. "They hate us," he agrees with Elshtain, because of who we are, answering the question George Bush posed in his address to Congress on September 20, 2001:

> Americans are asking, Why do they hate us? They hate what we see right here in this chamber—a democratically elected government. Their leaders are self-appointed. They hate our freedoms—our freedom of religion, our freedom of speech, out freedom to vote and assemble and disagree with each other.

Unlike "sophisticates," liberals, leftists, and especially postmodernists, Bennett, like Bush, knows evil when he sees it, and he's against it.

Accusing Others of Blaming America

As the war in Iraq approached, Bennett added a new preface to his book, called (without acknowledging Jeanne Kilpatrick's famous speech to a past Republican convention) "Blaming America First":

> There is a name for this attitude, and the name, once again, is anti-Americanism. In today's circumstances, in the face of an evil that only the United States can defeat, to hold this attitude is worse than irresponsible; it is a species of deep perversity. From the rest of us it requires a renewed response, one based on a true knowledge of our enemies and, especially, on a true knowledge of ourselves. This book is intended as a contribution to such knowledge.

Unless we utterly fail to grasp what the words "a true knowledge of ourselves" mean, his book fails to contribute anything to his or our self-knowledge. For all 9/11 seems to

The Insecurity of the Modern World Leads to Demonization and Terrorism

For the last thirty years America has been prone to a politics of demonization. The brutal attack on the World Trade Center reminds us, however, just how horrifying the end game of demonization can really be.

We argue that 21st century political resentments, rooted in the need to secure identity against anxieties about progress, globalization, life's purposes, and the imperative of economic growth create pressures that make demonization more likely. Temptations abound to increase the rancor we feel toward those who appear to adopt different solutions as they too negotiate these troubles. Thus categories of otherness harden and resentment may foster a politics comprised of contests between moral personae that easily devolves into demonization. An elusive fundamentalism is thus thrown into the mix of more obvious religious, cultural, ethnic or political forms (possibly reconfiguring them) presenting new possibilities for mutual harm, especially in an era of globalization marked by terrorism.

Tom De Luca, "Terrorism, Democracy, Globalization, and the Politics of Demonization," presentation, American Political Science Association meeting, August 2003.

have taught Bennett is that the "true knowledge" he always had is even truer today than when he set us straight before. Consider Bennett's earlier book *The Death of Outrage: Bill Clinton and the Assault on American Ideals* as he was driven to the edge by a public seemingly indifferent to Clinton's moral failure. It might please Bennett to know he has helped us find our outrage by suggesting that those who opposed the Iraq war, as we did, are "anti-American." Indeed, his book is mostly a diatribe designed to demonstrate that people who are unwilling to face the truth, which he knows with absolute certainty (e.g., that Iraq has stockpiled WMDs [weapons of mass destruction] to attack America), suffer from perversity. It might please him more to know that we have no postmodernist hesitation in judging his overall argument to be wrong, manipulatively structured, based on very selective if not distorted history and, well, to be bad. In fact, Bennett is a case study in what we have called the politics of moral personae. People who disagree with him are in turn wrong, evil, and perverse, an intellectualized/moralistic/pop-psych trifecta.

Attacking Nonjudgmentalism

Bennett's harshest words are reserved for postmodernists, relativists, intellectual sophisticates, and a variety of leftists and liberals. They either hate America directly, or they are studiously neutral about all ideas, actions, moral postures, or people, whether good or bad, which for him comes to the same thing:

> Subtly or crudely, nonjudgmentalism often serves as a mask for what can only be called judgmentalism of another and much worse kind. Summoning us to some all-embracing indulgence of the views of others, however wrong or evil, it encourages us, subtly or crudely, to deprecate the good when it happens to be ours—our own values, our own instincts, our own convictions, our own civilization. To put it another way, the refusal to distinguish good from evil is often joined with the doctrine that one society—namely the United States, or the West—is evil, or at the very least that it is to be presumed evil until proved otherwise.

Rejecting Tolerance

Unfortunately for Bennett he ignores an obvious implication of this general point. "All-embracing indulgence" in *his own views* masks injustice done by politicians and states *he* endorses, and obscures and distorts the views of his opponents.

He also writes as if the most common danger in human nature is too much tolerance, rather than self-love welded to power of the kind he advocates. He rightly asks: "Where was the peace movement [in the 1990s] while all this was going on, and was known to be going on? How could it sit idly by as a dictator acquired the means of mass destruction, the means to hold the whole world at bay?" Putting aside the hyperbole and inaccuracy (he wrote before the Kay report stating Iraq had no such weapons), how dare he make this charge and not even mention that the Reagan administration, in whose cabinet he sat, materially and deliberately supported Saddam Hussein and helped enable his depredations? The chemical weapons attack killing five thousand Iraqi Kurds in Halabja, Iraq, which Bennett himself cites and both presidents Bush adopted as a mantra—"he gassed his own people"—took place in 1988. Bennett is right that Hussein's regime and the man himself were simply barbarous, but they were the most barbarous when we supported them and looked the other way at their war crimes. With relativist aplomb, he has nothing to say on his own complicity with Saddam.

Fundamentalism of Left and Right

Bennett is not wrong about all he surveys. Some Americans on the left do have an instinctive dislike not just for policies of the American government, but also for American people and culture. Some postmodernists forget their debt to the modern commitments to dig deeply and to be rational, in ways that lead to moral dead ends, even as they remain harsh moral critics of people who don't agree with their point. Nor is Bennett alone. There are fundamentalisms, left, right, and center that adopt demonizing stances with structural similarities akin to Bennett's. Each of these postures inflames and thereby enables support for the others. They engage each other in a neurotic dialectic in which not just synthesis but respect is impossible.

After reading *Why We Fight*, we went to the Human Rights Watch Website. The horrors are there for all to see about Saddam Hussein; the facts are appalling. Did our own opposition to the war and the way it was unethically promoted make *us* insensitive to his evil, not wanting to know? Were we simply *unwilling* to give the administration the benefit of the doubt as to the reasons for war because of *who* the main advocate of war was? We always said had the Bush administration told us plainly that this was a war to *liberate* Iraqis, without the dissembling about WMDs and Al Qaeda, we would have given that view a fair hearing. But would we?

Closing Down the Discussion

Each Bennett of the world, whether on the left, right, or in the middle; modernist, postmodernist, or religious fundamentalist, instigates a process of closing down discussion, averting already polarized eyes from inconvenient facts. Each sounds a retreat into the sanctity of purified identity in the gear-up for total culture war. President Bush's rush to war under false pretenses made us angry. The worst offenders of the *culture* wars, however, are the clever intellectuals who ask, "Where is the outrage?" and then selectively deploy the question. Where *is* the outrage? For Bennett, it's where he feels like placing it. And not just in the terror war, but as warrior extraordinaire in the war for the soul of American culture.

Periodical Bibliography

The following articles have been selected to supplement the diverse views presented in this chapter.

Mariah Blake   "U.S. Culture War Moves to Europe," *Christian Science Monitor*, April 17, 2007.

Richard Crockatt   "No Common Ground? Islam, Anti-Americanism and the United States," *European Journal of American Culture*, September 2004.

Ricardo Duchesne   "Defending the Rise of Western Culture Against Its Multicultural Critic," *European Legacy*, August 2005.

Tony Gilland   "The Culture War Behind the Biotech Battle: How Irrational Fear Could Really Give Us Something to Worry About," *American Enterprise*, March 2004.

Eliza Griswold   "The Next Islamist Revolution?," *New York Times Magazine*, January 23, 2005.

Yossi Klein Halevi   "Culture War," *New Republic*, June 30, 2003.

Charles A. Kupchan   "Continental Woes," *Commentary*, September 2006.

Philip Marfleet   "The 'Clash' Thesis: War and Ethnic Boundaries in Europe," *Arab Studies Quarterly*, Winter/Spring 2003.

Richard Pells   "Culture Wars, Old and New," *Diplomatic History*, June 2003.

Alfred S. Regnery   "We Can Get Along," *American Spectator*, April 2004.

Deborah Scroggins   "The Dutch-Muslim Culture War," *Nation*, June 27, 2005.

George F. Will   "Paris Versus Philadelphia," *Newsweek*, October 10, 2003.

CHAPTER 4

Is the Culture War a Matter of Economics?

Chapter Preface

After nearly a decade of conservative, Republican ascendency in American politics, the culture war may be losing its ability to rally middle America around the party. In particular, less affluent Americans might be abandoning the free market policies favored by Republicans despite their agreement with that party on most of the culture war issues.

Traditionally, American politics was about economics; working class and lower middle class people tended to vote for the Democrats, while business owners, managment, and professionals favored the Republicans. The culture war changed that, as many blue collar people began voting for the Republicans, whom they saw as better representing the traditional values of family and hard work. The shift was particularly pronounced in the Southern, Midwestern and Western states. Workers' continual voting for the Republicans, despite the economic hardship many were undergoing, puzzled author Thomas Frank. In his book *What's the Matter with Kansas?*, he concluded that the Republicans were using the culture war to maintain power despite the apparent damage their free market policies have done to rural America. The liberal magazine *The Nation* applied Frank's idea to the 2004 election, noting that President Bush and Republican strategist Karl Rove used cultural issues to "distract Americans from their deepening credit card debt, rising healthcare costs and dwindling savings."

The Democrats lost in 2004 and Frank noted that "out in Red America, the right-wing populist revolt continues apace, its fury at the 'liberal elite' undiminished," but it may be that working-class voters heard Frank's message in 2006. That year's congressional election saw a shift back to economic concerns on the part of Red State Americans. Populist Democratic politicians such as Virginia's newly elected Senator James

Webb used the growing gap between the rich and the rest of the United States as an issue to counteract the Republican appeal to traditional values. His success might lead to a new phase of the culture war, one in which economic concerns combine with traditional values. Ironically, these new politics closely mirrors the old politics as practiced by the Republicans. The populists stress traditional values of family and patriotism (Webb himself is a Vietnam veteran), but note that working Americans are being hurt by free market policies originating in Washington, D.C., which benefit the wealthy of coastal cities like New York and Los Angeles.

Some traditionalist conservatives are also questioning the conventional conservative stress on free markets and economic growth at all costs. They decry the destruction of small town businesses by corporate giants such as Wal-Mart. They lament the loss of community in a society where young people in rural areas are often forced to leave their home towns to make a decent living. These traditionalists have gone beyond the usual conservative issues such as fighting gay marriage and abortion to pose questions about whether an unregulated *laissez-faire* economic system is truly good for American society. This new development (called Crunchy Conservatism by writer Rod Dreher) has led to a culture war on the right between free market conservatives and the traditionalists who are willing to see some government regulation.

It is possible that the near future will bring about a realignment in the culture war. Blue collar workers from the interior of the country may turn against conservative politicians, especially if liberal politicians are willing to subscribe to more conservative positions on social values. Conservatives themselves might split between those who value economic freedom above all and those who take a more holistic approach to what makes a stable community. The following articles offer a preview of how the culture war might shape up in the future.

> *"Conservatism provides its followers with a parallel universe, furnished with all the same attractive pseudo spiritual goods as the mainstream: authenticity, rebellion, the nobility of victimhood, even individuality."*

Conservative Politicians Use the Culture War to Mask Economic Problems

Thomas Frank

Thomas Frank is a cultural critic and the author of One Market Under God. *In this viewpoint, taken from his influential book* What's the Matter with Kansas?, *Frank portrays the contradictions that lead conservative small town voters to support policies that harm their economic interests. Frank believes that conservatives have convinced rural and small town people that liberal culture is corroding society. Thus despite the destruction that unchecked free market policies have done to small-town America, conservatives politicians still carry the day. Many in the culture industry, on the other hand, behave in ways guaranteed to alienate heartland voters, thus they play a part in ensuring conservative dominance.*

As you read, consider the following questions:
1. What are some of the symptoms of the economic decline of Frank's hometown?
2. How does the "culture industry" help to alienate small-town folk?
3. How do the real liberals Frank knows differ from 'liberals' as portrayed by *People* magazine or Hollywood?

In 1965, the year I was born, my family still lived in the blue-collar Kansas City suburb of Shawnee, a modest settlement on the westernmost perimeter of town, out beyond the tracks of the Santa Fe Railroad. It was a place where the city faded slowly into country, and the subdivisions were checkerboarded with soybean fields, and there were no trees tall enough yet to obscure the vast blue sweep of the Kansas sky. It was a "workers' paradise," my dad remembers now, a place where the ranch homes and split levels housed the families of appliance salesmen, auto mechanics, and junior engineers at the giant Bendix plant just across the state line: upbeat people, guys with GI Bill educations and color TVs in massive fake-mahogany cabinets. The world had not gone sour for them yet; had you told them then that they would one day be devoted to something like Fox News, a network that offers its viewers nothing but torture—endless images of a depraved world that, it tells them, they are powerless to correct—they would have questioned your sanity.

Shawnee today has the feel of a place whose energy has been spent, whose time has come and gone, like one of those dead towns built in the western half of the state in some burst of inexplicable optimism in the 1880s. When I visit the old neighborhood now, I am the only pedestrian on the streets, a spectacle so odd that people slow their cars down in order to get a better look at me. The elementary school my brother attended in the crew-cut days—B-47s roaring overhead as he capered on the jungle gym—is in the process of closing for good. There is not a trace of the armies of kids that used to chase one another up and down the blocks. Nor would those armies of kids be welcome in this new Shawnee, with its occasional heaps of rusting junk and its snarling rottweilers and its testy "No Trespassing" signs. The Lutheran church down the street that impressed five-year-old me with its daring sixties modernism looks today like a home-built A-frame, laughably shoddy, forlorn in a treeless lawn of knee-high weeds, its paint peeling. The shopping mall they were constructing the summer my family moved to Mission Hills has now passed through all the stages of retail life and is sinking irreversibly into blight, its storefronts empty except for a pool hall, a karate studio, and the obligatory "antique" store.

The implacable ideological bitterness that one finds throughout the state has here achieved a sort of saturation. The eastern part of Shawnee is still a blue-collar suburb, but after three decades of deunionization and stagnant wage growth, blue-collar suburbs like this one look and act very differently than before. Shawnee today burns hotter than nearly any place in the state to defund public education, to stamp out stem-cell research, to roll back taxes, and to abase itself before the throne of big business. The suburb is famous for having sent the most determined of the anti-evolutionists to the State Board of Education and for having chosen the most conservative of all Kansas state legislators, a woman who uses her hard-knock life story to dress up her constant demands that the state do whatever is necessary to lessen burdens on corporate enterprise. The offices of Kansans for Life, Tim Golba's old group, occupy a storefront in that dying mall, and the headquarters of the Phill Kline campaign are here

The Heartland Versus the Coasts

For more than thirty-five years, American politics has followed a populist pattern as predictable as a Punch and Judy show and as conducive to enlightened statesmanship as the cycles of a noisy washing machine. The antagonists of this familiar melodrama are instantly recognizable: the average American, humble, long-suffering, working hard, and paying his taxes; and the liberal elite, the know-it-alls of Manhattan and Malibu, sipping their lattes as they lord it over the peasantry with their fancy college degrees and their friends in the judiciary.

Thomas Frank, "What's the Matter with Liberals?"
New York Review of Books, *May 12, 2005.*

too, in a glorified Quonset hut squatting on a weed-covered lot three blocks from the former Frank residence.

A while back the *Wall Street Journal* ran an essay about a place "where hatred trumps bread," where a manipulative ruling class has for decades exploited an impoverished people while simultaneously fostering in them a culture of victimization that steers this people's fury back persistently toward a shadowy, cosmopolitan Other. In this tragic land unassuageable cultural grievances are elevated inexplicably over solid material ones, and basic economic self-interest is eclipsed by juicy myths of national authenticity and righteousness wronged.

The essay was supposed to be a description of the Arab states in their conflict with Israel, but when I read it I thought immediately of dear old Kansas and the role that locales like Shawnee play in conservatism's populist myth. Conservatism's base constituent, the business community, is the party that has gained the most from the trends that have done such harm out here. But conservatism's house intellectuals counter this by offering an irresistible alternative way of framing our victimhood. They invite us to take our place among a humble middle-American *volk*, virtuous and yet suffering under the rule of a snobbish elite who press their alien philosophy down on the heartland.

Yes, the Cons will acknowledge, things have gotten materially worse on the farms and in the small towns, but that's just business, they tell us. That is just the forces of nature doing their thing. *Politics* is something different: Politics is about blasphemous art and crazy lawsuits filed by out-of-control trial lawyers and smart-talking pop stars running down America. Politics is when the people in the small towns look around at what Wal-Mart and [agribusiness corporation] ConAgra have wrought and decide to enlist in the crusade against Charles Darwin.

But the backlash offers more than this ready-made class identity. It also gives people a general way of understanding the buzzing mass-cultural world we inhabit. Consider, for example, the stereotype of liberals that comes up so often in the backlash oeuvre: arrogant, rich, tasteful, fashionable, and all-powerful. In my real-world experience liberals are nothing of the kind. They are an assortment of complainers—for the most part impoverished complainers—who wield about as much influence over American politics as the cashier at Home Depot does over the company's business strategy. This is not a secret, either; read any issue of [liberal magazines] *The Nation* or *In These Times* or the magazine sent to members of the United Steelworkers, and you figure out pretty quickly that liberals don't speak for the powerful or the wealthy.

But when you flip through *People* magazine, you come away with a very different impression of what liberals are like. Here you read about movie stars who go to charity balls for causes like animal rights and the "underprivileged." Singers who were big in the seventies express their concern with neatly folded ribbons for this set of victims or that. Minor TV personalities instruct the world to stop saying mean things about the overweight or the handicapped. And beautiful people of every description don expensive transgressive fashions, buy expensive transgressive art, eat at expensive transgressive restaurants, and get edgy with an expensive punk sensibility or an expensive earth-friendly look.

Here liberalism *is* a matter of shallow appearances, of fatuous self-righteousness; it *is* arrogant and condescending, a politics in which the beautiful and the wellborn tell the unwashed and the beaten-down and the funny-looking how they ought to behave, how they should stop being racist or homophobic, how they should be better people. In an America where the chief sources of one's ideas about life's possibilities are TV and the movies, it's not hard to be convinced that we inhabit a liberal-dominated world: feminist cartoons for ten-year-olds are followed by commercials for nonconformist deodorants; entire families of movies are organized around some transcendent dick joke; even shows for toddlers have theme songs about keeping it real.

Like any industry, though, the culture business exists primarily to advance its own fortunes, not those of the Democratic Party. Winning an audience of teenagers, for example, is the goal that has made the dick joke into a sort of gold standard, not winning elections for liberals. Encouraging demographic self-recognition and self-expression through products is, similarly, the bread and butter not of leftist ideology but of consumerism. These things are part of the culture industry's very DNA. They are as subject to change by an offended American electorate as is the occupant of the Danish throne.

Never understanding this is a source of strength for the backlash. Its leaders rage against the liberalism of Hollywood. Its voters toss a few liberals out of office and are surprised to see that Hollywood doesn't care. They toss out more liberals and still nothing changes. They return an entire phalanx of pro-business blowhards to Washington, and still the culture industry goes on its merry way. But at least those backlash politicians that they elect are willing to do one thing differently: they stand there on the floor of the U.S. Senate and shout no to it all. And this is the critical point: in a media world where what people shout overshadows what they actually do, the backlash sometimes appears to be the only dissenter out there, the only movement that has a place for the uncool and the funny-looking and the pious, for all the stock buffoons that our mainstream culture glories in lampooning. In this sense the backlash is becoming a perpetual alter-ego to the culture industry, a feature of American life as permanent and as strange as Hollywood itself.

Even as it rejects the broader commercial culture, though, the backlash also mimics it. Conservatism provides its followers with a parallel universe, furnished with all the same attractive pseudospiritual goods as the mainstream: authenticity, rebellion, the nobility of victimhood, even individuality. But the most important similarity between backlash and mainstream commercial culture is that both refuse to think about capitalism critically. Indeed, conservative populism's total erasure of the economic could only happen in a culture like ours where material politics have already been muted and where the economic has largely been replaced by those aforementioned pseudospiritual fulfillments. This is the basic lie of the backlash, the manipulative strategy that makes the whole senseless parade possible. In all of its rejecting and nay-saying, it resolutely refuses to consider that the assaults on its values, the insults, and the Hollywood sneers are all products of capitalism as surely as are McDonald's hamburgers and Boeing 737s.

| "It can be perfectly rational to elevate
values above economic concerns."

Working Americans Value Both Self-Reliance and Community

David Callahan

The common perception is that in the last few decades, working-class white voters have become more conservative. Many liberals believe that these voters are being fooled into voting against their economic interests. In this excerpt from The Moral Center, *author and think-tank founder David Callahan makes the case that poorer voters are not being fooled when they vote to support free market policies. These policies reflect their belief in the value of work. Callahan argues that liberals should appeal to the American belief in just rewards for hard work, as well as the desire for community, in order to win back the working class.*

As you read, consider the following questions:

1. In the last 30 years, have working-class voters become more Republican throughout the United States? If not, in which region(s) have they become more conservative?

2. Why might economic concerns be less important than values to many poorer voters?

3. How does the free-market reinforce traditional values?

On Election Day 2004, George W. Bush won West Virginia by 13 percentage points. Bush's sweep of the state— where registered Democrats outnumber Republicans two to one—was impressive. In fact, Bush ran so strong in West Virginia that the Kerry campaign had written the state off well before November.

Exit polls told a familiar story about how Bush won. Voters with only a high school degree went for the president by a 17-point margin. Married voters favored him by 21 points; gun owners by 19 points. Bush performed best in the Appalachian Highland, one of the poorest parts of the state. He even won 41 percent of union members. The issue named most often at the polls was—you guessed it—"moral values"—and Bush won 88 percent of voters who said this was a primary concern.

The values question on the 2004 National Election Pool exit poll has been widely criticized as "poorly devised," preventing "meaningful analysis" of voter concerns, so it is hard to know what was on the minds of West Virginians. A more accurate analysis might well have found that national security was the dominant concern. We do know this: West Virginia is very conservative on social issues. Even many Democrats in the state are pro-life—so pro-life that the two Democratic congressmen from West Virginia each received a "0" rating from NARAL [National Association for the Repeal of Abortion Laws] in 2004. Those same Democrats got an "A" from the National Rifle Association. This is a land of traditionalism:

hard work in the mines, service to country when the call comes, a commitment to faith and family. The state's culture is deeply populist, making it fertile ground for the tirades of Rush Limbaugh or the homespun speeches of George Bush. The president's line about how the heart and soul of America wasn't in Hollywood went down particularly well here. . . .

Nothing drives liberals more insane than the belief that blue-collar Americans vote against their own economic interests. How can it be that working stiffs support millionaire Republicans who don't lift a finger on their behalf—and, in fact, are destroying their way of life? How could ordinary people be stupid enough to back politicians who feather the nests of fat cats while gutting things like education or health care? You could understand Joe Six Pack being fooled once or twice by some smooth-talking pol. But this has been going on for decades now.

Or has it? The political scientist Larry Bartels has shown that lower-income whites haven't actually become more Republican or more likely to vote based on social issues like abortion. Another political scientist, Jeffrey Stonecash, makes a similar case in his book *Class and Party in American Politics.* Both observe that the defection of working-class whites from the Democrats has been mostly confined to the South. Nationally, voting behavior now tracks more closely along income than in the past. Poorer voters more consistently vote Democratic; wealthier voters more regularly go for Republicans. Also, contrary to myth, poorer white voters do tend to see big differences between the political parties on economic issues, as well as on other matters.

Clearly the battle for the white working class isn't over yet; not by a long shot. On the other hand, poorer whites have never been a lock for the Democrats. In the eight presidential elections since 1972, only half of low-income whites voted Democratic on average. The other half were pivotal to GOP [Grand Old Party, the Republican Party] dominance.

Democrats Were Poised to Recapture Working-Class Voters Before the 2006 Congressional Election

[One type] of district where Democrats have a chance of unseating Republicans is white, working-class, and located in or near a mid-sized city like South Bend [IN] or Louisville [KY]. Voters in these districts tend to be less affluent, less educated, and more socially conservative. They are likely to be Catholics rather than evangelicals and to have had at least one family member who was, at one time, in a union. Many of them were Reagan Democrats who supported Clinton, but, after September 11, streamed back to the GOP because they believed Republicans were better equipped to wage the war on terrorism. These voters—and particularly white working-class women—provided the margin of Bush's 2004 victory in states like Ohio and Florida. But, distressed by the Iraq war, worried about gas prices and economic dislocation, and disgusted by Republican obeisance to K Street [The address of many Washington, D.C. lobbyists], they have begun to return to the Democrats.

John B. Judis, "Mood Indigo,"
The New Republic, *September 25, 2006.*

To win these voters, centrist Democrats have long argued that the party should tack to the middle on cultural issues, as Clinton tried to do. Others, such as author Thomas Frank, say that Democrats have lost the heartland because they abandoned economic populism. If liberals could revive that spirit—if they stopped flying Gulfstreams and driving Land Rovers, if they stood up for welders instead of whales, if they blew off Wall Street and got down with Main Street—poorer whites would come around.

This comeback plan has gained quite a bit of ground in liberal circles over recent years. It informed Gore's 2000 run, in which the former centrist vice president reinvented himself as a fire-breathing populist. "We're for the people, they're for the powerful!" Gore chanted. It was reflected in John Edwards's bid for the presidency, in which the onetime millionaire trial lawyer invoked a vision of "two Americas." And it is the solution offered by [Thomas Frank's book] *What's the Matter With Kansas?*, one of the most-read progressive tracts of recent times. If the liberal base of the Democratic Party has a clear vision of how to win power, economic populism is it.

It's easy to see the appeal of this vision. The crunch on low- and middle-income Americans is severe: unaffordable health insurance, stagnant wages, sky-high housing prices, inadequate child care. How long can Americans tolerate this abuse? Not much longer, I would think. In an age of insecurity, Democrats should be able to regain dominance by learning again to push the old economic buttons.

And maybe they can. But there are two problems here that liberals need to reckon with. One is that it can be perfectly rational to elevate values above economic concerns, even if you are not among the swells. If you're pro-life, you might well think that trying to stop over a million abortions a year is more important than getting a raise. If you're a parent, it might be reasonable to be more afraid of your teenage daughter getting pregnant or hooked on meth than losing your health coverage. If you're married, you could worry more about your spouse having an affair than your boss sacking you. Moral concerns like this are not nothing. Also, liberals vote their values all the time. No one asks, "What's the matter with Cambridge [Massachusetts, home of Harvard University]?"

The second problem is that in places like Kentucky and West Virginia, many liberal economic policies aren't much easier to sell than the theory of evolution. Democratic schemes to help the little guy often fall flat . . . with the little guy.

Now why is that?

I got one answer to this question when I traveled to Kentucky and met with Kent Ostrander, a leading conservative activist in the state. As Ostrander—an evangelical Christian—explained it, family values and economic conservatism go together naturally. Most social and economic challenges, he said, boil down "to the individual's duty to regulate himself." Liberals like to blame the system for everything, Ostrander said, while conservatives assume that individuals can make choices and act on those choices. This is true whether it comes to keeping a marriage intact or keeping food on the table. "If the individual cannot govern himself, then certainly the government is not going to be able to do it," Ostrander said.

A great many religious conservatives like Ostrander preach economic self-reliance, although scholars debate whether this holds as a general rule. The sociologist Stephen Hart has insisted that "religious traditionalism does *not* lead to economic conservatism," while another sociologist, Wayne Baker—echoing Max Weber—finds that if you're a traditionalist when it comes to family and religion, you're probably also a fan of the free market.

The truth may lie somewhere in between. The deeply traditionalist Catholic Church has issued strident calls for economic justice. Right-wing evangelicals, on the other hand, almost always back the GOP's fiscal conservatism. One possible reason that many evangelicals take such a tough stance on work and self-reliance is that their faith is very individualistic. Unlike Catholicism with its strict hierarchy, or mainline Protestantism, which can be very community oriented, evangelical Christianity stresses the personal dimensions of faith. If it's up to the individual to connect with Jesus Christ and find salvation, it's a small step to demanding that the individual also take full responsibility for their economic well-being.

Another view of why social and economic conservatism might go hand-in-hand comes from the linguist George Lakoff, who blasted out of obscurity not long ago to become a guru to Democratic leaders such as Nancy Pelosi [Representative from California]. In Lakoff's view, most conservatives subscribe to the "strict father model," which holds that we all need to learn self-discipline in order to be good and moral people—which means, among other things, delaying sexual gratification and honoring family commitments. A strict father teaches discipline to children by setting rules and meting out punishment. But the free market is another great disciplinarian, since everyone has to work hard to survive and work requires that you be responsible and diligent. Work means putting aside short-term desires, like the urge to sleep late or smoke a joint at lunch. The smaller the social safety net, the harder you'll work to keep your balance, exercising the self-discipline that leads to better behavior in other parts of life, such as marriage and family.

Thus the squared circle: Cutting social programs *helps* working families. Even someone who isn't doing so well might subscribe to this logic. . . .

The political scientist Jennifer Hochschild once commented that blind faith in the American Dream is unfounded, since plenty of people who work hard never succeed, but "it's all we have" and, like it or not, it will always be the dominant way we think about opportunity. Others have gone farther, arguing that the American Dream is the glue that holds America together in the absence of a common ethnic or national heritage. When a country is founded upon an idea, it's kind of hard to question that idea.

If that is true, and I think it is, it explains much. Liberals have a bad habit of contesting the premise of America. They say: No, opportunity doesn't exist for all, and no, hard work won't set you free. They offer a mountain of evidence to back up this view and assume these arguments will ring true given people's own life experiences. Instead, many Americans hear something else. They hear liberals trying to dash their hopes. Or they hear liberals talking down to them, pitying them for their difficulties and telling them they're in such bad shape that someone else needs to bail them out.

Republicans have seized on this mistake. They don't yet own the American Dream, but they've made a pretty good down payment on it in recent decades—whether through the "morning again" appeals of Ronald Reagan or the "ownership society" of George W. Bush. Republicans not only tell people they can take charge of their own destiny and be, in Bush's words, "truly free"; they have also typecast liberals as the enemy of such freedom, what with all their big-government schemes for taxes, red tape, zoning rules, class-action suits, hiring quotas, and so on. Liberals are for a Swedish nanny state, we're told, and have presided over the "death of common sense." Conservatives, on the other hand, embrace the frontier spirit.

Liberals haven't always been trapped in this corner. At various times their vision for economic freedom has trumped a narrower, laissez-faire notion of liberty. Liberals once championed the ideals of individual effort and responsibility—while also promising to tame market forces that fostered insecurity and a tyranny of the haves. Earlier liberals promised to make us free by giving each of us the ability to achieve our full potential. They blended themes of self-reliance with a moral insistence that America was a community and that we had to look out for one another.

Can this lost formula be rediscovered? I don't see why not.

| *"We are living in a time in which the image takes precedent over reality."*

Unbridled Capitalism Leads to Cultural Decay in the United States

Neal Wood

Neal Wood was a professor of history and political philosophy at the University of California Los Angeles and at York University in Canada. His books include A Trumpet of Sedition: Political Theory and the Rise of Capitalism. *In this viewpoint, taken from his posthumously published* Tyranny in America: Capitalism and National Decay, *Wood decries modern American consumerist society. The author holds that constant advertising leads Americans to pile up debt and disregard earlier values such as thrift.*

As you read, consider the following questions:

1. What are some reasons that consumerism might not lead to contentment?

2. How does the author connect advertising with rising personal bankruptcies in the United States?

3. How does the culture of advertising affect politics?

The United States is an inegalitarian class society generating a horrifying environment of crime and violence. Much of this seems to have resulted from advanced capitalism's ever expanding tyranny over our thoughts and activities. Capitalism appeals to and unleashes what used to be called the 'baser impulses' of humankind. Today, these baser impulses have been legitimized, are exalted, even eulogized, and promoted by every conceivable means at the disposal of the agents of capitalism's unregenerate tyranny. The emphasis, often ingeniously designed to avoid offending the squeamish, is invariably on the self, on enhancing the pleasure of the individual in the endless chase after money and possessions. No wonder a recent book by Marc Lewis, *Sin to Win*, should be doing so well in America. As reported in the *Financial Times* of 18 February 2002, Lewis maintains that 'self-interest is eternal—everybody always wants more'. He is of the opinion that 'vice is essential to success and no one should feel guilty about it. Coveting stops you being complacent.' Shades of Mandeville![1]

The Culture of Consumerism

The disease of consumerism has swept through capitalist America, impelled by advertising, the din of the mass media, the ease of borrowing. We are forever being urged to spend and spend, to buy and buy, to invest and invest. Americans, manipulated by the artful agents of capitalism, have been launched on an endless and mindless shopping and buying spree. The value of thrift, so cherished in the past, has been discarded. Americans, whether they can afford to or not, seem always to want more in a vain attempt to satisfy their endless desires. Personal satisfaction and contentment have long been forsaken, as fortunate Americans spend their earnings, often on useless commodities. Capitalism, people are constantly

---

1. Bernard de Mandeville, an eighteenth-century writer. In his "Fable of the Bees," he wrote that consumption, even over-consumption, could benefit society.

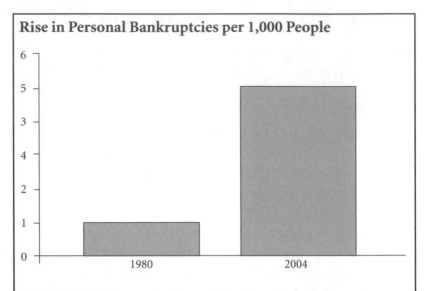

Rise in Personal Bankruptcies per 1,000 People

TAKEN FROM: Thomas A. Garrett, "Up, Up and Away: Personal Bankruptcies Soar." *Regional Economist, Magazine of the St. Louis Federal Reserve Bank*, October 2005.

warned, can only survive and thrive on the basis of perpetual spending and consumption. In their race to acquire more and more goods, many Americans seem to be ever unsatisfied. If America is a culture of class, a culture of violence, it is also a culture of consumerism. Everything and everybody have a monetary price, seldom related to their intrinsic worth. The value of everything depends on how much we desire it and are willing to pay for it. Everything and everybody are commodified, to be bought and sold in the market. To facilitate this shopping spree, shops are often open twenty-four hours a day, seven days a week, and Americans are serviced by nearly 30,000 shopping malls. Those who have computers can surf the Internet for the latest bargains in goods and services. Some, who perhaps can least afford it, are the psychological victims of shopping addiction, 'shopping crazy' in a literal sense.

More Bankruptcies

The penalty for the rampant consumerism is the rise of personal bankruptcy and indebtedness. Since 1970–80 bankruptcies have quintupled (in the past due to the relaxation of the law), approaching 1.4 million in 1997. The ratio of personal debt to income (after tax) grew from 59 per cent in 1984 to 83 per cent in 1998. American households apply an average of 17 per cent of disposable income to servicing their debts, just below the record high of 17.6 per cent in 1989. An average of $1,000 a year is spent on credit card interest and fees. The total household debt in 1998 has surged ahead to an astronomical $5.5 trillion. To satisfy further the insatiable demand of consumers, the total worth of imports far exceeds the exports, spiralling now to well over $20 billion a month, a forbidding problem that Americans will have to confront in the future. While congressmen are seriously considering a law requiring the display of the ten commandments in every school classroom in an effort to combat juvenile crime, and while much of the world's population struggles for the bare necessities of life, this circus of consumerism continues unabated.

Constant Advertising

Our very essence as humans is rapidly being reduced to the appetite for buying, as testified by the logo of a retailers' promotional organization: 'consume, therefore, I am'. The implications of this gross travesty of the famous Cartesian principle are horrifying. We exist not by virtue of our rationality, as [French Philosopher René] Descartes long ago argued, but because we have been reduced to mindless behavioural mechanisms programmed to the full to partake in a perpetual buying and spending spree. Christmas and Easter are now carnivals of consumerism with much touted 'store sales' tempting customers with a vast array of goods at bargain prices. Newspapers, magazines, TV, telephone, junk mail and flyers, and the Internet all turn life into a gargantuan bazaar. Commercials on TV bombard the viewer. In 1996, 15 minutes 21 seconds were allotted to 'non-programme' material in the average hour, up almost a minute from the previous year. Between a quarter and a third of every hour is devoted to commercial and promotional advertising. Although, during prime time, the viewer is confronted on average with twenty-seven commercials per hour, during the daytime this increases to forty commercials per hour, about one-third of every hour allotted to non-programme material. Built-in obsolescence of goods and constant changes in fashion ranging from clothing to motor cars and computers help fire consumer desire for ever more of the latest. Escape or respite from the constant display of advertising is virtually impossible even if we switch off our TVs and radios. Buses, taxis and even police cars are adorned with the most garishly colourful ads imaginable. Schools and even university lavatory doors are not immune to blandishments designed to entice new customers. Faced by the growing cutback of funds, some universities have resorted to finding corporate sponsors for courses, laboratories and lecture halls, the name of the business sponsor always given prominence. We are living in a time in which the image takes precedence over reality. Packaging and promotional drives, logos and brand names aim to fabricate a saleable appearance for commodities. Indeed voters elect specific candidates not on their merits or political programmes, but solely on the grounds of whose image projected on TV during their term of office would be the least boring and off-putting. Disneyland appearances seem to be confused with actuality. We are becoming the robots of virtual reality.

"I don't think conservatives have much of an answer for people who feel a sense of loss when 'progress' destroys beauty and authenticity."

Conservatives Must Look Beyond Free Market Values

Rod Dreher

In this viewpoint, Rod Dreher analyzes differences in worldview between what he calls "Crunchy Conservatives" and mainstream conservatives. Dreher is especially critical of the blind devotion to material "progress" and the free market that characterize today's conservatism. Dreher then goes on to point the blame at the media, especially television, for what he sees as the shallow materialism of American society. Unlike conventional conservatives, who rail against sex and violence on television, Dreher believes the problem is with the media's overall message which promotes continual acquisition of material goods. Rod Dreher is an editorial writer for the Dallas Morning Times.

As you read, consider the following questions:

1. How do "crunchy" conservatives and mainstream conservatives differ in their economic views?

2. How does television, and the media more generally, promote a culture of greed?

3. What are some of Dreher's symptoms of "media withdrawal?" What were some of the long-term benefits?

We on the right are big ones for saying that people need to get back to family values, or make room for God in their lives, or elect more Republicans to office. But this rarely moves beyond the level of rhetoric and sentimentality, and the fragmentation and alienation that cause us so much concern continue unabated, because we have not dealt with the root causes of our unhappiness. Our confusion comes in part because we don't recognize the disjunction between the ideals we profess to believe in as conservatives and the consumerist way of life we uncritically embrace.

Conservatives love to lecture liberals about the destructive quality of an ethic that justifies indiscriminate indulging of the sexual appetite. And we're right about that. But "thou shalt not covet" is a nonnegotiable divine command, too, and few are the conservative pastors who pound the pulpit to denounce acquisitiveness. Come to think of it, I've bored scores of priests in the confessional over the years with my sheepish tales of ordinary lust, but I could probably count on one hand the number of times I've thought to confess incidents of envy or greed. We on the right tend to think if we've kept our minds clean and our pants up, we're paragons of righteousness. But that's not true—not from an authentically religious point of view, and not from a traditionally conservative point of view.

The fundamental difference between crunchy conservatives and mainstream conservatives has to do with the place of the free market in society. Crunchy cons believe in the free market

Living a Lifestyle that Preserves Worthwhile Traditions

Slow Food practitioners work to preserve local culinary traditions and the conviviality of the traditional feast. Historic preservationists seek to restore living arrangements that encourage interaction rather than isolation. Homeschoolers shape their children's education around the eternal truths that are *verboten* in public schools. Conservationists protect the countryside for the sake of hunting and other wholesome enjoyments. The common thread running through these and other such efforts is the recognition of a precious patrimony that can only be squandered at the expense of the deep satisfactions that make life worth living.

Max Goss, "Crunchy Cons: The Good, the Bad, and the Annoying,"
Right Reason, *March 31, 2006. http://rightreason.ektopos.com.*

as an imperfect but just and effective means to the good society. When the market harms the good society, it should be reined in. Because crunchy cons, as conservatives, do not believe in the perfectibility or essential goodness of human nature, we keep squarely in front of us the truth that absent the restraints of religion, community, law, or custom, the commercial man will tend to respect no boundaries in the pursuit of personal gain. Absolute power corrupts absolutely, whether it's in the hands of big government or big business.

Crunchy cons believe mainstream Republicans have forgotten this. My favorite example comes from my friend Mike, who works in the home office of one of the most conservative Republican members of Congress. Because of his impeccable conservative credentials, Mike was appointed to the "smart-growth task force" of his city, whose putative task was to direct the city's residential and commercial development in a responsible way. At the first meeting, it wasn't long before Mike realized that the panel was merely a front for property developers.

"I made the observation that nowhere in the four-page [task force founding] document was there a mention of any possibility of any kind of restriction ever being placed upon development," Mike told me. "At which point the most vocal member of the task force, who also happens to be the most powerful developers' attorney in town and who represented a chain store's successful bid to steamroll a nearby community, cracked, 'This is a free-market conservative?'

"I pointed out that it wasn't my definition of a free market to see the highest-priced, best-connected attorney in town hired by a big corporation to make mincemeat of the simple neighborhood folk who resist their development; in fact, it seemed anti-democratic and anticonservative in its trampling of the individual and the community," Mike said.

It's telling that my friend wasn't merely opposed, but denounced as a fake conservative because he opposed business interests. That, I'm afraid, is what so much mainstream conservatism amounts to nowadays: whatever serves the interests of commerce is baptized as conservative. That's pathetic.

Bryan Greer, a crunchy con from Northfield, Minnesota, wrote me to say, "I don't think conservatives have much of an answer for people who feel a sense of loss when 'progress' destroys beauty and authenticity. Conservatives can only mumble about the necessity of economic progress. They don't seem to care that something of real value has been lost."

Bryan said he's a lifelong Republican, but he's afraid for Republicans to take over his town's government because he doesn't trust them to conserve the character of the town center. Which is another way of saying the Republicans in his town were capitalists first, conservatives second. [Economist E. F.] Schumacher spoke to this point when he observed that in today's economy, "anything that is found to be an impediment to economic growth is a shameful thing, and if people cling to it they are thought of as either saboteurs or fools."

What drives this destructive materialism? Good old greed and envy, mostly, which are always and everywhere present, and which can be combated by moral exhortation and reform. But there is something else working to drive the materialist dynamo, something so basic to our way of life that few even think to question it, something so ever present that to propose resisting it is to present yourself as a latter-day King Canute, ordering the incoming tide to turn around and head back to sea.

I'm talking about technology.

Neil Postman, the late media critic, was a man of the left, but he is beloved by the crunchy right for his incisive analyses of how mass media and technology undermine cultural and social institutions that make for good societies. He delivered perhaps his most radical critique of contemporary culture in his 1992 book *Technopoly*, which depicts American society as having structurally surrendered its soul and its liberty to technology. The word "structurally" is important, because in Postman's view, we have constructed our economy, our society, and even our way of seeing reality to serve technology. Americans naïvely accept new technologies, thinking only of what these technologies can do, but never, said Postman, what they can *undo*.

Consider television, and the way it conditions us to interpret reality. Now, whenever conservatives get their dander up about TV, it's almost always to rant about salacious programming. *Run for your lives, it's Janet Jackson's unsheathed ta-ta!* Postman said this kind of thing is a pointless distraction, that those who complain about the content of programming "are like the house dog munching peacefully on the meat while the house is looted." He invited us to think more deeply into how the medium itself changes the way we think.

By its very nature, television technology teaches us to experience the world as a series of fragmentary images. It trains us to prize emotion and stimulation over logic and abstract thought. We are conditioned to expect quick resolution to problems, and to develop evanescently short attention spans. We expect the world to be entertaining if it is to hold our attention; eventually, we learn to judge the world by essentially aesthetic criteria. For the man who gets his metaphysics from television, boredom is the root of all evil. As media critic Read Mercer Schuchardt told me, "Morality today is very point-and-click; life is completely about image and surface texture now." . . .

I used to be a TV critic, actually, and finally got so bored with it that I quit my job and moved into a country house down South to put myself through media detox and figure out what to do with my life. I spent the fall and winter of 1993 living virtually alone there, with no television, no newspaper, and no Internet (I did have a radio, and got my news from NPR). All I had was books, silence, and solitude.

The withdrawal was difficult. I was jittery and easily distracted. The monastic quiet unnerved me. But gradually I reconciled myself to it, and came to love it. There was no buzzing in my head anymore. I found I could write long letters, and sit for lengthy stretches reading novels. Prayer became easier. I started living by the rhythm of the day, awakening at daylight, and going to sleep not long after the sun went down. I began to feel, well, normal. I discovered how to be alone with my thoughts, and in turn how to think in a sustained way. Had I ever known how to do that?

By the end of my four months at that house, I felt vastly less anxious, restored to myself, and I had learned to listen for life's quieter, deeper sounds drowned out by the daily media cacophony. That was a decade and a half ago, and many times since then I have wished I could pack up my family and move to a place like that, where we could live the tranquillity of a media-free existence.

| *"The West has never been comfortable
with its own cultural vulgarity."*

Free-market Culture Gives People the Liberty They Crave

Charles Paul Freund

In this viewpoint, Charles Paul Freund, a senior editor at Reason magazine, argues that consumerism is an expression of freedom. While many cultural critics look down at mass popular culture created to meet the demands of the free market, Freund sees it as disruptive, shaking up the social order and breaking down the limits imposed on individuals and groups historically considered to be "outsiders." Rather than seek to limit capitalist cultural production, those who believe in liberty and democracy should praise it.

As you read, consider the following questions:

1. How did the Afghans celebrate their liberation from the Taliban? Why did this upset some Western cultural critics?

2. According to Freund, how does consumerism help individuals create their own identities?

Charles Paul Freund, "In Praise of Vulgarity: How Commercial Culture Liberates Islam—And the West," *Reason*, vol. 33, no. 10, March 2002, pp. 24–35. www.reason .com. Copyright © 2002 by Reason Foundation, 3415 S. Sepulveda Blvd., Suite 400, Los Angeles, CA 90034. Reproduced by permission.

3. What are some examples in the article of "moral panics" over things which have since become widely accepted?

Who will ever forget the strangeness of the first images out of post-Taliban Afghanistan, when the streets ran with beards? As one city after another was abandoned by Taliban soldiers, crowds of happy men lined up to get their first legal shave in years, and barbers enjoyed the busiest days of their lives.

Leonardo DiCaprio Invades Kabul

Only a few months earlier, in January 2001, dozens of barbers in the capital city of Kabul had been rounded up by the Taliban's hair-and-beard cops (the Ministry for the Promotion of Virtue and Prevention of Vice) because they had been cutting men's hair in a style known locally as the "Titanic." At the time, Kabul's cooler young men wanted that Leonardo DiCaprio look, the one he sported in the movie. It was an interesting moment in fashion, because under the Taliban's moral regime movies were illegal, Leonardo DiCaprio was illegal, and his hairdo, which allowed strands of hair to fall forward over the face during prayer, was a ticket to jail. Yet thanks to enterprising video smugglers who dragged cassettes over mountain trails by mule, urban Afghans knew perfectly well who DiCaprio was and what he looked like; not only did men adopt his style, but couples were then celebrating their weddings with Titanic-shaped cakes.

DiCaprio was out of style, even in Kabul, by the time the Taliban's rules were being swept away along with the nation's beard clippings. Men were now measuring their freedom by the smoothness of their chins. "I hated this beard," one happy Afghan told an A. P. [Associated Press] reporter. Being shaved was "like being free."

Cigarettes as Freedom

Although it's omitted from the monuments and the rhetoric of liberation, brutal tyrannies have ended on exactly this note before. When Paris was liberated from the Nazis, for example, one Parisian cadged a Lucky Strike from an American reporter, the first cigarette he'd had in a long, long time. As he gratefully exhaled, the Frenchman smiled and told the reporter, "It's the taste of freedom."

Afghan women, of course, removed their burqas, if they chose to, and put on makeup again. But some Afghan women had been breaking the morals laws throughout the period of Taliban bleakness; according to a memorable CNN documentary titled *Beneath the Veil,* they did so at the risk of flogging or even amputation. Courageous women had not only been educating their daughters in secret, but had also been visiting illegal underground cosmetic parlors for the simple pleasure of self-ornamentation and the assertion of self-fashioned identity that lies behind it. . . .

Other Afghans exhumed the TV sets they had buried in their yards to save them from the autos-da-fé of electronics the Taliban staged in Kabul's soccer stadium. A few Afghans examined the homemade satellite dishes—hammered out of old paint cans—that were arrayed in the streets. Those who didn't have TVs anymore ran out to see what they could get from sellers who had put their black market stocks of electronics on open display. The shoppers were looking for a boom box or for any machine that would help return pleasure to their lives.

In short, the first breath of cultural freedom that Afghans had enjoyed since 1995 was suffused with the stuff of commercially generated popular culture. The people seemed delighted to be able to look like they wanted to, listen to what they wanted to, watch what they wanted to, and generally enjoy themselves again. Who could complain about Afghans' filling their lives with pleasure after being coerced for years to adhere to a harshly enforced ascetic code?

The West's liberal, anti-materialist critics, that's who.

The High Culture Sputter

"How depressing was it," asked Anna Quindlen in a December *Newsweek* column, "to see Afghan citizens celebrating the end of tyranny, by buying consumer electronics?" Apparently, if you're somebody like Quindlen—who confessed in the same column that "I have everything I could want, and then some"—the spectacle was pretty dispiriting. Liberty itself descends on the land, and the best thing its people can do is go shopping? It was just too vulgar.

There are a lot of sputterers like Quindlen, and they too condemn the substance of Afghanistan's national liberation celebration. Why? Because they think that cultural consumerism—whether nascent as displayed in Kabul or full-blown as in the hedonist West—is the serpent in freedom's garden. When culture and commerce meet, they believe, both democracy and prosperity are poisoned. As for true culture, it hasn't got a chance.

Influential Critiques

Hence, when Hillary Clinton, then still the first lady, addressed the World Economic Forum in Davos, Switzerland, a couple of years ago, she argued that "there is no doubt that we are creating a consumer-driven culture that promotes values and ethics that undermine both capitalism and democracy." In fact, she said, "I think you could argue that the kind of work ethic, postponement of gratification, and other attributes that are historically associated with capitalism are being undermined by consumer capitalism."

Leave aside the spectacle of making such a speech to some of the world's richest and most privileged people gathered in a highly exclusive Alpine resort. Clinton's message was actually a restatement of a well-known and highly regarded thesis. She'd lifted her text straight out of Daniel Bell's classic 1974 study *The Cultural Contradictions of Capitalism*. Capitalism was built on an ethic of work and duty, Bell argued, but it yields a culture of self-involved pleasure that undermines the attitude necessary for disciplined achievement.

The man of the hour at this nexus of culture, democracy, and commerce, however, is Benjamin R. Barber, a political science professor now at the University of Maryland. As cultural darkness descended on the Afghans, Barber published a 400-page sputter called *Jihad vs. McWorld: How Globalism and Tribalism are Reshaping the World* (1996). His argument was that tradition-bound, often blood-based anti-modernism ("Jihad") is one of two powerful forces in the world undermining true democracy. The other rogue force? "Unrestrained capitalism," especially of the sort displayed by aggressive, resource-depleting, soul-destroying multinational corporations ("McWorld"). Their encounter, he argued, would explode at the expense of the noble communitarian ideal of civil society. Barber's tome was illustrated with a striking image of a woman clad in a black burqa holding a can of Pepsi, the Western drink of "choice" throughout most of the Arab and Islamic world. . . .

In other words, the confluence of markets and culture has repeatedly advanced democratic values, because it has allowed a series of outgroups—women, blacks, Jews, gays, etc.—successfully to address the larger society about injustice and inequality. Such appeals have been successful precisely because of their "vulgar" forms. It is because they have involved such emotionally compelling forms as music and melodrama that they have induced their audiences to experience a given injustice through the eyes of those suffering from it. Justice's medium is empathy, and empathy's medium is more often the melodrama than it is the manifesto. In short, it is the broad-

Secular Commerce Paves the Way for Religous and Other Freedoms

If there is hope for freedom and decency in the world, it is in secular commercial culture. Religions and the religious especially should sing the praises of secular commercial cultures, for they especially benefit.

If this seems counter-intuitive, it's no surprise. We're told quite loudly and often that America is a Christian nation, strong and successful (according to half of the population) only because it has been especially blessed with the Judeo-Christian tradition. But the real blessing of the American way is one that atheists or Buddhists can share just as surely as the most devout evangelical Christian.

Brian Gongol, "In Praise of Commercial Culture,"
Gongol.com, May 29, 2005.

based culture that emerges from markets that frequently serves as a means of democratic self-correction.

Blaming the Culture Industry

Capitalism's critics in the West blame what they call "the culture industry," which makes itself rich by aggressively manipulating consumerist idiots. The latter part with their money because they have been persuaded that some truly useless but expensive object will make them hip, youthful, or desirable, or raise their status. This manipulative scheme is now a global enterprise, filling the world with what Benjamin Barber and his ilk castigate as "junk." Worse, say the Daniel Bells and Hillary Clintons, it's a threat to Western prosperity, because it instills self-absorption at the expense of the work ethic.

This critique completely misses the point of cultural commerce. The citizens of the post-subsistence world have a historically remarkable luxury: They can experiment with who they are. They can fashion and refashion their identities, and through much of their lives that is just what they do. They can go about this in a lot of ways, but one of the most important methods is what is known and reviled as "consumerism." They experiment with different modes of self-presentation, assert or mask aspects of their individuality, join or leave a series of subcultures, or oppose and adhere to centers of power. It is from this complex mix that the things of the material world become the furnishings of both a social and a personal identity. That's what meaning is.

Consumerism of this sort has been born and reborn many times. The extended and apparently open-ended chapter in which the Western world has been wallowing began in 17th-century Britain, Holland, and other European trade centers. It is still being reborn all over the world, as people grab the first opportunity to escape the traditionalist boundaries of selfhood. Yet this is the very spectacle that depresses the West's anti-consumerist critics and makes them sputter. . . .

Popular Culture Is Disruptive

The West has never been comfortable with its own cultural vulgarity. Such anxiety is arguably strongest in the United States, which has long nursed a cultural inferiority complex vis-à-vis more-established British and European practitioners of high art. Popular, commercial forms are not thoughtful. Rather, they are temporary, noisy, intense, ecstatic. They are sensual and disruptive. Because they are frequently set in motion by powerless and even despised outgroups, they appear subversive. They not only threaten social morals, but challenge established power relationships.

The result is that such ecstatic forms are attacked not only by the West's left-liberal critics for their commercial origin, but by the West's conservatives for their disruptive power. Cultural ecstasy may have billions of participants, but it hardly has a single friend.

For the last 200 years, vulgar forms and subcultures have often set off a series of "moral panics" among those who perceive a threat to their own cultural power and status. The popular novel, when it first appeared, set one off. So did penny dreadfuls and pulps. So did melodramatic theater. So did the music hall. So did the tabloid press, and the waltz, and ragtime, and jazz, and radio, movies, comic books, rock music, television, rap, and computer games.

All of these—and more—led contemporary critics to declare the end of civility, to worry over some newly identified form of supposed "addiction" (to novels, to TV, to video games, to pornography, to the Internet, to Pokémon, etc.), to announce that the coming generation was "desensitized," and to rail about childishness and triviality. It's the cultural sputter that never ends.

Suppressing Vulgarity

In democratic societies, most such panics simply run their course until the media tire of them. (Drug prohibition remains a singular exception.) Thus, the generation that in the 1950s was dismissed as Elvis-loving, hot-rod-building, gum-chewing, hog-riding, leather-wearing, juvenile-delinquent barbarians eventually achieved a mature respectability in which the artifacts of their vulgarity became sought-after nostalgia, and even a beloved part of the common cultural heritage. In less than two decades, the menacing hoods of *Blackboard Jungle* became the lovable leads in *Grease*. By then, however, that same generation had become, in its turn, concerned about the disruptive social effects of rap music and violent electronic gaming.

In places where the moral order is the legal order, however, ecstatic forms and assertive ways of being remain matters for the police. In December, Cambodia's prime minister ordered tanks to raze the country's karaoke parlors. Last fall, Iran announced a new campaign against Western pop music and other "signs and symbols of depravity." And only last summer, the Central Asian Republic of Kazakhstan—just a few hundred miles north of Afghanistan—began a crackdown on dangerous "bohemian" lifestyles. The authorities went after a number of familiar outsiders—gays, religious dissidents— but even Westerners were surprised to learn that one targeted group was "Tolkienists." It turns out that there are Kazakh Hobbit wannabes who like to dress up in character costume and re-enact scenes from J.R.R. Tolkien's novels. For their trouble, they were being subjected to sustained water torture.

Hobbit re-enactors in Kazakhstan? Where do they get their paraphernalia? Are there Kazakh Tolkienist fanzines? Have fans started changing Tolkien's narratives to suit themselves, the way Western *Star Trek* subcultures turned their own obsession into soft-core pornography? Do re-enactors change roles from time to time, or are any of them trapped inside a Frodo persona? Is there no end to the identities waiting to be assumed? No end to what invention makes flesh, before it tosses it aside and starts again?

> "Rural America is becoming the target
> of a new wave of 'ethical' policies,
> which urge us to boycott American
> farming on grounds that reflect the life-
> style choices of the urban elite."

There Is a Culture War over the Countryside

Roger Scruton

Roger Scruton is a British conservative commentator, writer, and philosopher. In this viewpoint he disparages the left-leaning British Labour government's policies toward the English countryside. Scruton maintains that Labour draws few votes from England's farming regions and that the urbanites who lead Labour have no feeling for the traditional way of life in the country. One consequence was the campaign to ban hunting with dogs, a traditional activity of the rural English. Scruton does not see the same disdain for rural life in the United States, but he warns of a creeping campaign to impose the values of city sophisticates on American farmers and ranchers.

As you read, consider the following questions:

1. According to Scruton, why does the British left wish to transform the countryside?

Roger Scruton, "Countryside and Culture," *American Spectator*, vol. 39, no. 7, September 2006, pp. 52–54. Copyright © 2006 the *American Spectator*. Reproduced by permission.

2. Why does Scruton disparage the "Countryside Agency" created by Britain Labour government?

3. How do American views of the countryside differ from British views?

There is an emerging "Culture War" which has dominated British politics for the last two decades, and is beginning to be noticeable in America too, and that is the war over the countryside.

The Dangerous Countryside

How should the land be settled? For what purpose, by what kind of people, and with what way of life? Things go on in rural America that have come to the attention of the elite. Reports from visiting missionaries speak of environmental mischief, of primitive rituals with animals, of grotesque outbursts of patriotism, and of the frightening emergence of a "Christian Fundamentalist Right." There are whole swathes of the country without vegetarians or public homosexuals, and where the principal amusements are bear hunting, pig wrestling and rodeos. The urgent desire to police this moral wilderness is therefore beginning to make itself felt in the suburbs, and it may be time for American conservatives to observe what has happened in Britain, where the countryside has for a long time occupied the debating columns of the weekly journals, dictated much of the agenda of public radio, and been the conscious theme of a continuous stream of novels and documentaries.

The question of the countryside has also been the only question of interest to the Labour Party over the last decade, and the only question towards which the British government has a coherent policy. Labour members of Parliament took up a record 220 hours of parliamentary time in order to force through the bill banning "hunting with dogs," while devoting only 18 hours to the war in Iraq. And it was clear from the beginning that the debate was not about animal welfare but about culture—specifically about the culture of Old England, with its hierarchical social order, its equestrian way of life, and its carefully woven landscape of fields, hedgerows, and quaint little villages, so offensive to the "multicultural" orthodoxies of the new ruling class.

The symbolic significance of hunting with hounds was revealed when the government, in response to worries about Welsh and Scottish devolution,[1] established a website inviting people to propose their favorite icon of England. When it became clear that hunting was coming out on top—way ahead of football and fish and chips—it was removed from the site. Protests from the Countryside Alliance (a pressure group formed to represent rural England) led to its restoration, not as hunting but as "hunting and the opposition to it," so that pictures of hunt saboteurs in their balaclava helmets could feature alongside the proud uniforms of the Beaufort and the Berkeley [hunts] as symbols of the England we love.

Bureaucratization of Rural Life

So deep is the New Labour obsession with the countryside that the government has established a "Countryside Agency" to oversee the abolition of this cultural thorn in its side. It was an explicit requirement that the chairman of the agency should be an opponent of hunting, and it soon became clear that the ideal candidate would be a visitor to the countryside, who flees back to the city appalled by the primitives who shoot rabbits, keep ferrets in cages, have no need of social workers, and attend their local church. The job went to a bureaucrat who lives in Birmingham and who gained his experience of the English countryside at the World Bank, the IMF [International Monetary Fund], and the Treasury. Meanwhile, the agency has been filled with appointees with no reputation

---

1. Limited self-rule for Wales and Scotland, two of the "nations" of the United Kingdom.

in the countryside except as people who would like to abolish it, while the new minister for rural affairs—David Miliband— lives in London and confesses that he does not own a pair of Wellington boots. His principal cultural significance is that he is the son of Ralph Miliband, one of the most poisonous of the Marxist gurus of the 1960s.

The target of New Labour's antagonism remains today what it was for 19th-century radicals: the landed gentry who, notwithstanding the fact that they have lost their land and are no longer gentry, remain the main hate figures in British left-wing demonology. Had the ancestral sport of the landed classes been golf rather than hunting we should have certainly seen moves to outlaw golf. But golf is an approved use of the countryside, being the favorite sport of urban incomers. More-over, golf courses mutilate acre upon acre of those irritating pastures and establish car parks and clubhouses in the place of ancestral halls. Yet more politically correct is "rambling"— the habit of escaping from the city in order to trample over other people's fields. One of the most important laws passed by New Labour conferred the "right to roam" over large tracts of rural England, regardless of the rights of those who are the nominal owners. And two aggressive ramblers now sit on the board of the Countryside Agency, pursuing their campaign to abolish all private ownership of Britain's coastlines, so that the louts of modern Britain can expose their flaccid torsos on ev-ery beach in the land.

The attack on the English countryside and its culture is also a reaction to the Second World War. In those difficult years the family farm became the symbol of continuity, settle-ment, and national sovereignty. It was an icon which, thanks to [painters John] Constable and [George] Stubbs, [writers Robert] Surtees and [Anthony] Trollope, [composers Edward] Elgar and [Gustav] Holst, was already fully articulate in the English mind. Those great artists lived in a world of tranquil husbandry, in which social hierarchies were largely undis-

turbed, and troubles were exported across the seas. Hunting
was an unquestioned part of the rural life that they celebrated,

a kind of ritual repossession of the landscape in the name of the tribe. Wartime propaganda films from Ealing Studios therefore dwelled upon farming and country life, and when [poet T. S.] Eliot produced his great response to war in the Four Quartets, it was to rural England and its gentle religion that he turned for inspiration.

The American View of the Countryside

Although the founding fathers were landed gentry in the English mold, their way of life has never been resented by the American people. Nor has the countryside acquired any settled cultural significance for the majority of Americans. There have been important agrarian movements, which have found expression in the arts. But the art, literature, and music of rural America are as egalitarian and democratic as the art, literature, and music of the cities. The countryside has somehow failed to become a symbol either of wealth or of social hierarchy, even though it can be as rich and hierarchical as any region of rural England. Hostility to rural America is therefore largely directed at farmers, and at their rough and dominating ways with the natural world. Environmentalists look on the American farm as a disaster. Campaigners for "fair trade" and "global justice" urge that food should not be produced at home but imported from the small farmers of Africa and South America. Activists for "animal rights" press for legislation to control every aspect of farming, to restrict or abolish hunting, and to ensure that our relation to other species conforms to the Disneyfied rituals that tie urban people to their imprisoned pets. In short, rural America is becoming the target of a new wave of "ethical" policies, which urge us to boycott American farming on grounds that reflect the lifestyle choices of the urban elite.

A new book by Peter Singer and Jim Mason, *The Way We Eat: Why Our Food Choices Matter*, portrays exemplary members of this elite, who show their contempt for America and its lifestyle in their ability to weep at the touch of a button over America's transgressions and who symbolize their sensitive natures in the food that they eat. We follow them on their daily visits to the organic food market, stand over them as they cook their beans and sorghum, and listen to the tedious moralizing that only people like themselves, living at one remove from production and enjoying all the hidden subsidies of the modern suburb, can afford to act upon. Their "ethical" suppers are symbols of a deep conviction—shared by a growing number of American liberals—that the countryside is in the wrong hands.

The End of Country Life

For the British leftist, the countryside needs to be taken over by the urban crowds and trampled to extinction. Better a sterile wilderness than the Eden of the old upper class. The American liberal has a more positive approach to the problem. His goal is a suburban jungle, with people carefully slotted into the spaces between habitats, moving on tiptoe through the territories of raccoons and bears, and living on an imported diet of "fair-trade" vegetables. Either way the countryside will contain no conservative voters, and say no prayers to the Christian God. And either way, it will cease to produce what the country needs in peacetime, so preparing the way for instant surrender in time of war.

Periodical Bibliography

The following articles have been selected to supplement the diverse views presented in this chapter.

Joseph L. Conn	"Rift on the Right," *Church & State*, April 1999.
David Dark	"The Misfits," *Christian Century*, June 13, 2006.
Rod Dreher	"A Green Christian Conservative," *USA Today*, April 24, 2006.
Thomas Frank	"Why They Won," *New York Times*, November 5, 2004.
Jonah Goldberg	"Living in the Real World," *National Review*, March 27, 2006.
Christopher Hayes	"The New Democratic Populism," *Nation*, December 4, 2006.
Gertrude Himmelfarb	"The Election and the Culture Wars," *Commentary*, May 2000.
Joe Klein	"The Democrats' New Populism," *Time*, July 2, 2006.
Gilbert Meilaender	"Hold the Granola," *First Things: A Monthly Journal of Religion & Public Life*, May 2006.
Thomas A. Moser	"Protecting the Environment," *Modern Age*, Winter 2005.
Nation	"Kulturkampf, 2004," March 22, 2004.
Bruce Pilbeam	"Natural Allies? Mapping the Relationship between Conservatism and Environmentalism," *Political Studies*, October 2003.
Katha Pollitt	"Let's Not Devalue Ourselves," *Nation*, August 16, 2004.
Chris Weinkoft	"A Community of Faith," *American Enterprise*, May 2006.

For Further Discussion

Chapter 1

1. Robert Reich maintains that the culture war is alive in twenty-first century America, while Jonathan Rauch disagrees. Based on your reading of their viewpoints, which author is more correct in describing the cultural climate in the United States today? Support your argument with examples from the viewpoints.

2. Domenick Maglio blames the culture war on "rich elitists" who are undermining traditional morality, while David A. Horowitz thinks that politicians stoke cultural clashes by scapegoating government bureaucrats. Which group do you believe is stoking the culture war: elites in the media and academia or politicians seeking votes? Think of some examples from your own reading to support your answer.

Chapter 2

1. Humanists, or secular progressives, believe that religion should be kept out of all government activities. Can you think of a setting where prohibiting a display of religion might actually interfere with religious liberty? What are some occasions in school activities where religious beliefs might be expressed? Should such expressions be banned?

2. Conservatives or traditionalists often claim that excluding religion from the public sphere is to deny America's tradition as a religious nation. What are some examples from David Limbaugh's viewpoint supporting the idea that teaching American history without religion distorting history? Can you think of counterexamples that show religion was relatively unimportant to America's founders?

3. An important recent controversy in public education has
    been the teaching of intelligent design as an alternative to
    Darwin's theory of evolution in science courses. Barbara
    Forrest and Glenn Branch believe this is a backdoor way
    of sneaking the religious docrine of creationism into the
    science curricula. Do you think that public schools should
    be required to present alternatives to conventional scien-
    tific theories? How much and what type of evidence of
    support should be required before an alternative to a con-
    ventional scientific theory can be taught in public schools?

Chapter 3

1. Christine Odone's viewpoint makes the case that, in Brit-
    ain, religious believers from differing faiths (e.g., evan-
    gelical Christians and Muslims) are making alliances to
    fight a dominant secular culture. George Weigel is not
    optimistic about such alliances; he believes that Muslims,
    with their growing numbers, will dominate rather than
    cooperate with Christians. Do you think interfaith alli-
    ances are stable in the long term? Why or why not? Sup-
    port your answers with examples from the viewpoints and
    from your own knowledge.

2. Stanley Kurtz notes a new "population bomb"; in many
    advanced countries (especially in European countries and
    Japan) couples are not having enough children to replace
    themselves, leading to a shrinking population. What spe-
    cifically might countries do to increase their birthrate?
    How, according to Kurtz's argument, might these policies
    lead to a conservative shift in society? Do you believe
    that a smaller population is all bad, or might there be
    some benefits? Brainstorm examples of possible advan-
    tages and disadvantages of a smaller population.

3. Bill O'Reilly believes that secularist progressives hinder
    government security measures and thus assist terrorists
    who would attack us. How would Tom De Luca and John

Buell characterize O'Reilly's statements? Do you believe
O'Reilly is raising legitimate concerns? Why or why not?

Chapter 4

1. According to Thomas Frank's viewpoint, Republican politicians have been able to blind heartland voters to their
   economic woes by characterizing themselves as protectors
   of traditional values. Do you believe most voters vote on
   financial issues, or on "values" issues? Give some examples of "values" issues which might have led
   traditionally-minded voters to vote for Republicans even
   against their economic interests.

2. Thomas Frank believes that economic policy and traditional values are at best not connected, at worst just rhetoric to fool voters into supporting conservative politicians.
   David Callahan's viewpoint is in part a response to this
   idea. How does Callahan show that traditional family values are connected with economic well-being? Give some
   examples from his viewpoint and from your own knowledge.

3. For the past three decades, conservatism has been associated with free-market, pro-business economics. According
   to Rod Dreher's viewpoint, why might unconditional support for the free-market undermine traditional values?
   How does "consumerism" serve business interests? What,
   according to Charles Paul Freund, are the benefits of consumerism? What are some basic differences in the two
   authors' ideas of a good society? Give examples of consumerism from the viewpoints.

Organizations to Contact

The editors have compiled the following list of organizations concerned with the issues debated in this book. The descriptions are derived from materials provided by the organizations. All have publications or information available for interested readers. The list was compiled on the date of publication of the present volume; the information provided here may change. Be aware that many organizations take several weeks or longer to respond to inquiries, so allow as much time as possible.

Acton Institute for the Study of Religion and Liberty
161 Ottawa NW, Suite 301, Grand Rapids, MI   49503
(616) 454-3080 • fax: (616) 454-9454
e-mail: info@acton.org
Web site: www.acton.org

The Acton Institute is dedicated to promoting its view of religious liberty, which is from a general libertarian, Roman Catholic perspective. The group's activities lean toward the intellectual rather than toward policy activism. Its Web site features information about its many programs as well as an electronic version of its journal *Markets and Morality*.

American Civil Liberties Union
125 Broad Street, 18th Floor, New York, NY   10004
(212) 549-2500
e-mail: aclu@aclu.org
Web site: www.aclu.org

The ACLU is a national organization that works to defend the rights guaranteed by the United States Constitution. Its primary work is to support court cases against government actions which violate these rights, including matters of private morality and separation of church and state. The ACLU also publishes and distributes policy statements, pamphlets, and the semiannual newsletter *Civil Liberties Alert*.

Americans United for Separation of Church and State
518 C Street NE, Washington, DC   20002
(202) 466-3234 • fax: (202) 466-2587
e-mail: americansunited@au.org
Web site: www.au.org

The AU, in 2007, celebrated sixty years of fighting to preserve the distinction between politics and religion in the United States. The group's Web site is a source for the history of religious liberty in the United States, as well for media briefings on current issues of concern to the AU. Those who support the AU's views can sign an online petition available at the site.

Anti-Defamation League
823 United Nations Plaza, New York, NY   10017
(212) 490-2525
Web site: www.adl.org

The ADL works to stop the defamation of Jews and to ensure fair treatment for all United States citizens. It publishes the periodic *ADS Law Report* and *Law Enforcement Bulletin* as well as reports addressing specific issues.

Carsey Institute
73 Main Street, Huddleston Hall G05B
The University of New Hampshire
Durham, NH   03824
(603) 862-2821 • fax: (603) 862-3878
e-mail: carsey.institute@unh.edu
Web site: www.carseyinstitute.unh.edu

The Carsey Institute at the University of New Hampshire is devoted to investigating issues of concern to rural America. The institute publishes detailed reports as well as briefer media materials in order to facilitate a national dialog on policies affecting families in America's hinterland. Recently, the Institute published a report, available on its Web site, on the disproportionate number of American casualties in Iraq suffered by rural and small town communities.

Cato Institute
1000 Massachusetts Avenue NW
Washington, DC   20001-5403
(202) 842-0200 • fax: (202) 842-3490
Web site: www.cato.org

The Cato Institute is a libertarian public policy research foundation dedicated to individual liberty, limited government, free markets, and peace. The Institute publishes the online journal *Reason*, the bimonthly *Cato Policy Report*, and numerous books.

The Center for Rural Strategies
46 East Main Street, Whitesburg, KY   41858
(606) 632-3244 • fax: (606) 632-3243
e-mail: info@ruralstrategies.org
Web site: www.ruralstrategies.org

The Center for Rural Strategies focuses on improving rural life by increasing public knowledge about America's rural communities. The group's efforts are mainly devoted to media relations and informational campaigns, serving as a conduit to convey information about the American countryside to the public at large. Their Web site features links to videos and a blog covering rural life.

Christian Coalition of America
P.O. Box 37030, Washington, DC   20013-7030
(202) 479-6900 • fax: (202) 479-4260
e-mail: coalition@cc.org
Web site: www.cc.org

The Christian Coalition bills itself as "the largest and most active conservative grassroots political organization in America." It focuses on voter education to reach citizens whom it feels will endorse its pro-life, pro-family agenda. In particular, the Christian Coalition mails out tens of millions of voter's guides and newsletters to let Americans know various candidates' positions on issues such as abortion, education, and taxes.

The Council on American-Islamic Relations
453 New Jersey Avenue, SE, Washington, DC   20003
(202) 488-8787 • fax: (202) 488-0833
e-mail: info@cair.com
Web site: www.cair.com

CAIR's mission is to promote understanding of Islam, protect civil liberties, and to empower American Muslims. The council engages in lobbying, education, and advocacy on the behalf of followers of Islam in the United States. Recent efforts have been focussed on the prevention of profiling of Muslims during the U.S.'s War on Terror.

Foundation for Individual Rights in Education
601 Walnut Street, Suite 510, Philadelphia, PA   19106
(215) 717-FIRE (3473) • fax: (215) 717-3440
e-mail: fire@thefire.org
Web site: www.thefire.org

FIRE is dedicated to ensuring the free speech rights of students and educators. The organization concentrates on legal work to ensure that campuses are places of free inquiry and debate of ideas both conservative and liberal.

Heritage Foundation
214 Massachusetts Avenue NE, Washington, DC   20002-4999
(202) 546-4400 • fax: (202) 546-8328
e-mail: info@heritage.org
Web site: www.heritage.org

The Heritage Foundation is a conservative think-tank which is devoted to economic opportunity, prosperity, and a flourishing civil society. The group opposes growth of government and supports what it sees as traditional American values of family and economic independence.

The Humanist Society
1777 T Street NW, Washington, DC   20009-7125
(800) 837-3792 • fax: (202) 238-9003

e-mail: info@humanist-society.org
Web site: www.humanist-society.org

The Humanist Society is dedicated to promoting knowledge of humanism and aiding humanists in their daily lives. They are advocates of a strict separation between church and state. Their Web site features the electronic magazine *Humanist Living*, as well as links to other groups advocating humanism.

People for the American Way
2000 M Street NW, Washington, DC   20036
(800) 467-4999 • fax: (202) 467-4999
e-mail: pfaw@pfaw.org
Web site: www.pfaw.org

People for the American Way is dedicated to preserving civil liberties, especially in the area of religious freedom. The organization fights against the encroachment of religion into public institutions. It engages in both legal action and lobbying lawmakers.

Traditional Values Coalition
100 S. Anaheim Boulevard, Suite 350, Anaheim, CA   92805
(714) 520-0300 • fax: (714) 520-9602
e-mail: mail@traditionalvalues.org
Web site: www.traditionalvalues.org

The Traditional Values Coalition's mission is to empower people of faith through knowledge. It is especially concerned with matters of family and sexuality and opposes government policies which it sees as undermining traditional morality in these areas.

Bibliography

Books

Nijole V.
Benokraitis, ed.
Feuds about Families: Conservative, Centrist, Liberal, and Feminist Perspectives. Upper Saddle River, NJ: Prentice Hall, 2000.

John R. E. Bliese
The Greening of Conservative America. Boulder, CO: Westview Press, 2001.

Tammy Bruce
The Death of Right and Wrong: Exposing the Left's Assault on Our Culture and Values. Roseville, CA: Forum, 2003.

Tammy Bruce
The New American Revolution: Using the Power of the Individual to Save Our Nation from Extremists. New York: William Morrow, 2005.

Ira Chernus
Monsters to Destroy: The Neoconservative War on Terror and Sin. Boulder, CO: Paradigm Publishers, 2006.

Ann Coulter
Godless: The Church of Liberalism. New York: Crown Forum, 2006.

Dinesh D'Souza
The Enemy at Home: The Cultural Left and Its Responsibility for 9/11. New York: Doubleday, 2007.

Morris P. Fiorina with Samuel J. Abrams and Jeremy C. Pope | *Culture War?: The Myth of a Polarized America.* New York: Pearson Longman, 2005.

Bruce Fleming | *Why Liberals and Conservatives Clash.* New York: Routledge, 2006.

Joshua D. Freilich and Rob T. Guerette, eds. | *Migration, Culture Conflict, Crime and Terrorism.* Burlington, VT: Ashgate, 2006.

Eric T. Freyfogle | *Agrarianism and the Good Society: Land, Culture, Conflict, and Hope.* Lexington: University Press of Kentucky, 2007.

Norton Garfinkle and Daniel Yankelovich, eds. | *Uniting America: Restoring the Vital Center to American Democracy.* New Haven: Yale University Press, 2005.

Lloyd Geering | *Fundamentalism: The Challenge to the Secular World.* Wellington, NZ: St. Andrew's Trust for the Study of Religion and Society, 2003.

Jim Geraghty | *Voting to Kill: How 9/11 Launched the Era of Republican Leadership.* New York: Simon and Schuster, 2006.

Bernd Hamm, ed. | *Devastating Society: The Neo-Conservative Assault on Democracy and Justice.* Ann Arbor, MI: Pluto Press, 2005.

James Davison Hunter | *Before the Shooting Begins: Searching for Democracy in America's Culture War.* New York: Free Press, 1994.

James Davison Hunter and Alan Wolfe — *Is There a Culture War?: A Dialogue on Values and American Public Life.* Washington, D.C.: Brookings Institution Press, 2006.

Susan Jacoby — *Freethinkers: A History of American Secularism.* New York: Metropolitan Books, 2004.

Peter Knight — *Conspiracy Nation: The Politics of Paranoia in Postwar America.* New York: New York University Press, 2002.

Frederick S. Lane — *The Decency Wars: The Campaign to Cleanse American Culture.* Amherst, NY: Prometheus Books, 2006.

Norman Lebrecht — *Covent Garden: The Untold Story.* Boston: Northeastern University Press, 2001.

Jeff Lewis — *Language Wars: The Role of Media and Culture in Global Terror and Political Violence.* Ann Arbor, MI: Pluto Press, 2005.

Brian Mann — *Welcome to the Homeland: A Journey to the Rural Heart of America's Conservative Revolution.* Hanover, NH: Steerforth Press, 2006.

Arthur McCalla — *The Creationist Debate: The Encounter between the Bible and the Historical Mind.* New York: T & T Clark International, 2006.

John Harmon
McElroy

Divided We Stand: The Rejection of American Culture since the 1960s. Lanham, MD: Rowman and Littlefield, 2006.

Elizabeth Anne
Oldmixon

Uncompromising Positions: God, Sex, and the U.S. House of Representatives. Washington, DC: Georgetown University Press, 2005.

W. Mark
Richardson and
Gordy Slack, eds.

Faith in Science: Scientists Search for Truth. New York: Routledge, 2001.

Jonathan Rieder
and Stephen
Steinlight

The Fractious Nation? Unity and Division in Contemporary American Life. Berkeley: University of California Press, 2003.

Ralph William
Sarkonak

France/USA: The Cultural Wars. New Haven: Yale University Press, 2001.

Tom Sine

Cease Fire: Searching for Sanity in America's Culture Wars. Grand Rapids, MI: W. B. Eerdmans, 1995.

Gordy Slack

The Battle Over the Meaning of Everything: Evolution, Intelligent Design, and a School Board in Dover, PA. San Francisco: Jossey-Bass, 2007.

Ben Stein and
Phil DeMuth

Can America Survive?: The Rage of the Left, the Truth, and What to Do about It. Carlsbad, CA: New Beginnings Press, 2004.

Kenneth D. Wald
and Allison
Calhoun-Brown

Religion and Politics in the United States. Lanham, MD: Rowman and Littlefield, 2007.

Adam Kempton Webb   *Beyond the Global Culture War.* New York: Routledge, 2006.

Index